Fear and L
Reactions

the DESIGN MUSEUM

Fear and Love
Reactions to a Complex World

Edited by Justin McGuirk
and Gonzalo Herrero Delicado

Foreword
Deyan Sudjic

Design – so designers have been telling themselves since at least the days of William Morris – is an essentially optimistic activity. 'Have nothing in your houses that you do not know to be useful and believe to be beautiful,' as Morris suggested. To design is to consider how we might make the world a better place in which to live. It is an aspiration that is ambiguous enough to cover both the utilitarian and the spiritual definition of the subject. But there are other views. Victor Papanek, for example, was a notable dissenter. He wanted to divorce design and designers from business. There were, he conceded, some activities that are more dangerous than industrial design, but precious few of them. Papanek distrusted styling as no more than a means to manufacture want. Papanek's reputation has grown as we have tilted away from the celebrity-driven, brand-led design culture that eclipsed him even before he died, and embraced a more serious-minded commitment to confronting the ills that threaten us. The idea of authorship, of creative self-expression, is nowadays not as popular with students as more collaborative approaches.

We live in an age of anxiety, and complexity. We can see that design and designers may have played a part in creating some of those anxieties. We fear that the planet is in danger from our ever-expanding impact on it. We fear that machines and artificial intelligence may threaten our species. We fear the ever-increasing pace of change – and we fear the loss of self, and of privacy, caused by technology. To argue that designers have had a hand in this is not an act of self-aggrandizement. It is a reflection of the part that designers play in making technology useable, and so in driving change. And design is a means of offering solutions as well as of amplifying potential problems.

Fear and Love, the exhibition with which the Design Museum opens its new home in Kensington, acknowledges these anxieties. But it is rooted in optimism. Design today may be more questioning than it has sometimes been, but it is still about making possibilities. Against a background of extraordinarily rapid change, this is an exhibition which uses design to explore the challenges that face us, and the ways in which we might address them. And at the most fundamental level, it is an assertion of the continuing significance of design.

Design must operate in the midst of constant flux. The Design Museum first opened at the beginning of the 1980s, three years before mobile phones finally managed to cut loose from the coiled plastic bonds that tethered them to the insides of cars, and escaped into the street when Nokia sold its first Mobira Cityman (at a retail price of £4,000). In an early marketing initiative it gave one to the leader of the Soviet Union. In the thirty years since, Nokia grew to dominate the world market for an entirely new category of product, and then all but vanished as it was eclipsed by other communications devices. And the Soviet Union has gone altogether. At every level, the world has been transformed: politically, socially, technologically and culturally. In 1983, there was no internet, or at least not as we know it, and the digital revolution had yet to show itself. Ettore Sottsass, a designer and architect who successfully managed to combine the pursuit of the utilitarian and the spiritual in design, caught the attention of the world with what seemed to some to be a baffling onslaught on the conventional idea of what design should be. He switched his attention from designing elegant typewriters for Olivetti to the Memphis group, which explored the potential of design to convey meaning. At that time, it seemed like an existential challenge to the idea of taste, and production logic. From the perspective of the present, Sottsass's work with Memphis seems as firmly rooted in the continuing history of design as does that of William Morris.

Against that background, we worry about the ways in which what we once saw as certainties now seem in doubt. Has the pace of events rendered old definitions of what design can be no longer relevant? Have we been looking at the map upside down? Have we even been looking at the wrong map?

The underlying message of *Fear and Love* is that we have a remarkably varied and rich set of responses available to us from design and designers. These are responses that can help us make sense of what is happening to the world, and that also offer us ways of making the most of the possibilities that they offer. Design for every generation might seem to be about different things, but at heart it is still about our values, about the choices that we make and about how we make possible their realization.

Introduction
Justin McGuirk

Every age has its fears. In ours, the list is long and growing longer. Annual fear surveys are becoming as much a marker of contemporary society as the 'basket of goods', the group of consumer products used to track rising prices. The Chapman University in California has structured its annual survey into ten 'domains of fear'.[1] These include: Technology (from robots taking our jobs to online fraud); Environment (global warming and pollution); Natural Disasters (earthquakes and floods); Man-made Disasters (terrorism); Personal Future (lack of financial security); Government (immigration and drones); Judgement of Others (appearance and gender identity); and, of course, Crime. Readers will no doubt identify with at least a handful of these – they are rehearsed daily in the newspaper headlines.

The very notion of tracking our fears suggests that they are subject to change. Implicit in the results, however, is the idea that one of the root causes of our fear is change itself. We live in an age that is changing faster than any before it. As the sociologist Zygmunt Bauman has argued in a series of books – including *Liquid Love* (2003) and *Liquid Fear* (2006) – we inhabit 'a liquid modern world known to admit only one certainty – the certainty that tomorrow can't be, shouldn't be, won't be like it is today'.[2]

Design has long been one of the forces driving and reflecting that fluid flow of change. Design makes change tangible. It is written across the cultural and industrial production of the twentieth century – every shift in technology, taste and behaviour is manifest in some product or building, some piece of fashion or typography. But what this book and the accompanying exhibition argue is that design itself is changing. It is not restricted to a world of objects and artefacts. Even if *things* are still design's primary and most visible output, it is increasingly implicated in less tangible materials.

It is now a banal truism to point out that many of the products we once took for granted – cameras, calculators, calendars, watches, books and maps – have disappeared behind a touchscreen, absorbed into the digital realm. But within this culture of the immaterial – of the virtual – design is also operating on a much broader and deeper plane. The rise of planetary-scale systems, from software to network infrastructure, means that design is now fundamental to the operating systems, if you will, of twenty-first-century life. That fact weaves design into many of the fears alluded to above – questions of trust, privacy, resilience, security, even survival.

The rapid pace of technological change makes our products ever more disposable. And, though we are well aware that design has consequences, and that every product exists within a system of resource extraction and waste, we feel helpless to stop the flow

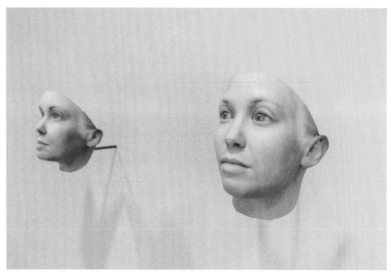

Radical Love, a 3D portrait of Chelsea Manning created by Heather Dewey-Hagborg in 2015 using forensic DNA phenotyping. The portrait challenges the notion of fixed genders.

of goods into landfill sites. Indeed, we are starting to worry that our technological prowess may challenge what it means to be human. From wearable technology to genetic engineering and synthetic biology, we are beginning to blur the edges between the *natural* body and the man-made. We witness the social fallout of rapid urbanization, and the rampant inequalities of a billion people living in slums. In short, design is inextricably bound up with many of the pressing issues of our day—and they are nothing if not *emotive* issues. They cause fear, and addressing them will require, yes, ingenuity but also optimism, hope, compassion—let's call it love.

The traditional rhetoric of design is so reasonable, so rational. It is a measured language of appropriateness—form must follow function; design must solve problems. Where emotions are involved, they are concerned with desire and attachment, with possessiveness. But design today is playing a bigger game with higher stakes than just consumer sales figures. It is widely accepted that design has a role to play in tackling the major issues of our times, from the environmental crisis to the symptoms of rampant inequality. Shouldn't the discourse embrace pathos? Can we allow ourselves to speak of repressed emotions, to give vent to the irrational? *Fear and Love* is an atmosphere, a mood. It taps into an ineffable feeling that life is less stable and predictable than we remember and that epochal challenges lie ahead of us, if only we could stand to look them in the face.

The Geometry of Fear
The present, however, has no monopoly on anxiety. One only has to think back to the mid-twentieth century, with Europe in ruins and the threat of Mutually Assured Destruction (MAD) from nuclear weapons hanging over the planet. Those real and potential horrors were reflected in the art of the day. The group of British sculptors, including Lynn Chadwick and Eduardo Paolozzi, who exhibited at the Venice Biennale in 1952 came to be known by Herbert Read's memorable phrase 'the geometry of fear', their tortured forms representing an 'iconography of despair'.[3] Only a year earlier, though, the Festival of Britain had heralded an altogether more optimistic era. It was a time for rebuilding, for modernizing. It was a celebration of British design and manufacturing, and a testament to a nation's can-do spirit. Artists were still processing, still asking why. Design's role, by contrast, was to look forward, to change, to be ever optimistic. And, of course, that is still design's assigned attitude to this day. The idea that design might be implicated in the causes of fear, bound up in the enervating churn of change, goes against the discipline's self-image.

Introduction

The Ooho, an edible form of water packaging made from algae, was designed by three students from the Royal College of Art in 2014 to demonstrate that there are alternatives to polluting plastic bottles.

Throughout history, humanity has feared what it did not understand or could only partially grasp. Succumbing to diseases or the cruel forces of nature could only be attributed to God or fate. But design, as it emerged out of the Industrial Revolution, was a by-product of the Enlightenment project, which sought to shed light through reason and to banish irrational fears. Design was part of the mastery of nature, the shaping of forces and materials to a prescribed plan. Through standardization and mass production, we were able to equip ourselves for a better life. That project culminated in the certainties of Modernism, with its emphasis on light and hygiene, on repeatable, machine-made forms that allowed *good design* and standardized housing to lift the masses out of squalor.

This capacity of design to 'solve problems' was synonymous with progress. Though consumerism is now much maligned, in the early and mid-twentieth century one could genuinely argue that the mass production of consumer goods was linked to growing social mobility and improved living conditions on a scale never before seen. It would be much more difficult to make that case for the Western society of today, where social mobility is falling and the future prospects of the youth are more uncertain than they were a generation ago. The market for design goods is so saturated that the innovations necessary to drive sales merely load products with baroque levels of functionality that are surplus to requirements.

And yet, the technologies of the network age offer one paradigm shift after another. As Lee Vinsel and Andrew Russell have argued, 'progress' has been replaced by 'innovation' – 'a smaller, and morally neutral, concept'.[4] While Silicon Valley has revolutionized the way we communicate, the very way we mediate the world, its innovation fetish pretends to be socially liberating but instead chains us to ever-faster cycles of change and obsolescence while creating natural monopolies for the tech elite. 'Innovation provided a way to celebrate the accomplishments of a high-tech age without expecting too much from them in the way of moral and social improvement,' write Vinsel and Russell. The establishment has bought into 'disruption', which is more exciting than maintenance, and consequently US public infrastructure is crumbling.

The modernist faith in progress has assumed an archaic, fairy-tale quality. Today, our technical facility is as much a cause of anxiety as of hope. Bauman argues that our tools have a logic that develops independently of our best interests. The example he gives is the atomic bomb, which US President Harry S Truman dropped on Hiroshima not because it was necessary to win World War II but because it was there – the US had invested millions and millions of dollars in the bomb, and it could not go to waste. In other

　　　　　　　　　　　　　　Justin McGuirk

Yakubu Al Hasan, one of a series of portraits by Pieter Hugo at Agbogbloshie e-waste dump in Ghana, 2009

words, it was not rational. And the same might be said of the fearsome tools we are developing today, from data-gathering systems to artificial intelligence. They have their own ineluctable trajectory.

Rather than relieving our anxiety, design and technology are as likely to engender it. The fear of not keeping up, the fear of missing out (FOMO), the fear of smouldering e-waste dumps in Ghana, the fear of plastic gyres in the oceans, the fear that robots will take our jobs and that drones will surveil us from the skies while our smart gizmos surveil us at home. We fear the ominous weather, the rising sea levels and the superbugs breeding in our modern hospitals. Medicine, technology and design were supposed to solve problems, not create them. They were supposed to banish fear.

Instead, we are back in a world where the systems are too vast and complex to understand, and too entrenched to be reversible. Our atavistic fear of nature has become the fear of what humans have done to nature. Global warming and the Anthropocene—the consequences of globalized industrialization—have gone from threats to facts, and the natural disasters are coming in evershorter cycles. We are back in the realm of irrational fears—the fear of that which we can only partially grasp.

And just what, I hear you ask, has love got to do with it? The idea is not as outlandish as it may sound. Historically, design has had two modes: eliciting desire—through beauty—and 'solving problems'. In modernist dogma, those two modes were supposed to be indistinguishable. But throughout history—whether we are talking about medieval craftsmen or the design professionals who emerged after the Industrial Revolution—design's role has been to make us love our objects. Just as Charles Darwin argued that the decoration of plants and animals was at the root of sexual selection, so the decoration or beautification of objects is aimed at seducing us, the potential owners of those things. Design aspires to make us feel desire, or at least some kind of emotional attachment. And while no one would limit design in such terms, it is clear that our attachment to certain facets of the modern lifestyle represents a problem. Put a different way: the sources of our fear are the things that we love. These things may be convenience, fashion or cheap consumer goods—all of which have environmental and social consequences. We do not just have a fear problem, we have a love problem.

This love has fetishistic qualities, as anyone who has ever camped outside an Apple store the night before a product launch should know. A decade before the Spike Jonze film *Her* (2013), in which a man falls in love with his phone's operating system, Bruce Sterling described the mobile phone as a 'relationship machine'. In *Tomorrow Now* (2002), he wrote, 'The sexy hardware is merely

In Spike Jonze's film *Her*, 2013, the hero falls in love with his phone's operating system – the perfect illustration of the phone as a 'relationship machine'.

a come-on; the relationship [with the service provider] is what matters.'[5] In a networked world where seemingly everyone and everything is connected, these relationships are as much design's terrain as the enticing object. Beauty is just a means to an end. And so the *love* we talk about in this book is more than mere attraction or attachment.

If design is to operate in an expanded mode – in a way that can tackle the so-called 'wicked problems' of our time – it will have to cut deep into emotional territory. As a humanist discipline, design is well versed in the love and passion that designers put into their work. The resurgence of craftsmanship as an ideal, for example, has something to do with the fact that it reminds us of our humanity, and our appreciation may be bound up with such Ruskinian notions of the maker's happiness or fulfilment. But even this is a kind of self-love. The kinds of love that design might tap into are more akin to compassion: togetherness, cooperation, mutual understanding – the will to improve life, and not just our own, the will to nurture and protect our habitat. *Love*, that most mawkish and sickly of words, encompasses the range of emotional responses required: creativity, optimism and hope.

The Contemporary Sublime

In the eighteenth century, Enlightenment philosophers such as Edmund Burke and Immanuel Kant turned to the concept of the sublime to account for aesthetic experiences for which 'beauty' was simply inadequate. Alpine peaks were sublime precisely because they were fearsome, awe-inspiring sights that made one all too aware of one's physical and mental limitations. Unlike beauty, which had a defined form, nature's marvels were terrifying because they were 'boundless', too large to comprehend. In the twenty-first century, the sublime is more likely to be man-made than natural. In the early stages of discussing this exhibition, the speculative designers Dunne and Raby proposed displaying the designs for a man-made high-tech mountain – a satirical critique of the 'moonshot' ambitions of today's tech giants. And while it remained merely a proposal, not long afterwards Tony Dunne sent a link with the headline 'United Arab Emirates considers building man-made mountain to increase rainfall'. Such a feat, were it achieved, would be in line with any number of spectacular landscapes that have been geo-engineered, from Dubai's Palm Island to opencast mines that spiral deep into the earth. But these are all too tangible.

Today, the sublime has resurfaced in technological form. As the architect and theorist Lars Spuybroek writes, 'Would it be legitimate

Justin McGuirk

Inside a Supernap data centre in Nevada, USA

Map of internet usage generated as part of the Opte Project by Barrett Lyon in 2010

to direct all the questions we had concerning nature in the early 1800s ... at technology? At some point technology and nature have switched positions.'[6] There is an argument to be made that the technological sublime is the new mountain. We struggle to imagine the planetary-scale networks that support our lifestyles or to comprehend the near-magical properties of our devices, and so we give them metaphorical names such as 'the cloud'. And Spuybroek, though he critiques the notion of a technological sublime, conjures a connected world in which such fears are highly tangible: 'Every technical object seems to have the power to expose us, to make us vulnerable, because it immediately turns into an occasion or event that links us to others.'

Design has a role in both shaping and communicating the systems that keep the world turning, whether we are talking about flight paths, electrical grids, internet networks or stock-market trading algorithms. We rely more and more on complex but fragile systems in which the slightest glitch can have tragic consequences. These systems manifest themselves in forms that range from the sublime to the mundane. One of the icons of early internet-era data visualization was the maps of internet usage created by Barrett Lyon, which resembled microscopic spores or dandelion seeds. One of them graced the cover of Bruce Mau's 2004 book *Massive Change* (which, since we are discussing the boundlessness of the sublime, was created in collaboration with his Institute Without Boundaries). If we are honest, those maps communicated little other than complexity in a pretty form, and so perhaps their purpose was merely to give shape to the ungraspable. At the more pedestrian scale, the writer and designer Dan Hill recounts an anecdote about being caught in a rain shower in London and, after buying an umbrella for £2, being forced to ponder what fiendish globalized system could possibly deliver such an intricate product into his hands for so little money.[7]

The notion that design operates at the systemic level and not just in objects is not new. In 1963, Richard Buckminster Fuller argued for the 'Comprehensive Designer', a non-specialist who could stand apart from industry and be able to observe the potential for creating useful tools without creating unbalanced systems. This designer would be 'an emerging synthesis of artist, inventor, mechanic, objective economist and evolutionary strategist'.

Similarly, Herbert Simon claimed that 'Everyone designs who devises courses of action aimed at changing existing situations into preferred ones.' Arguing that design education was too 'cookbooky' (a complaint still made today), Simon advocated the more technocratic 'science of design', with a focus on cybernetic-style

Superstudio's series of collages, *Supersurface*, 1972, imagined a world of total communication that anticipated the network age.

problem solving. And Lucius Burckhardt, teaching at that bastion of *gute form*, the Hochschule für Gestaltung at Ulm, could argue that design is invisible and shapes every institution, from hospitals to seemingly natural phenomena such as night-time: 'Thus the night, which evidently originally had something to do with the dark, is a man-made construct, comprised of opening hours, closing times, price scales, timetables, habits and streetlamps.'[8]

Today's complex systems are both designed and integral to the way design is evolving. Ours is a 'platform' culture that allows individuals scattered across the globe to interact in real time. Open-source systems, whether facilitating software or products, have revolutionized the design process, allowing anyone to modify or customize the outcome. The so-called 'hive mind' – again we draw our metaphors from nature – and the distributed manufacturing that it enables is disrupting the traditional control of designers and manufacturers. In some ways, it is the return of a utopian spirit to design – a world not of copyright and outsourced mass-manufacturing but of shared intelligence and localized micro-production.

Increasingly these man-made systems mirror the complexity of nature. We produce micro-robots that swarm; we create networks with autonomous qualities. One such is blockchain, which powers the cryptocurrency bitcoin. Blockchain, a distributed database that remembers every transaction run through it, is the kind of new organizational structure that in theory could replace traditional institutions such as banks. In the real world, the architecture that supports our networked culture is some of the largest and strangest ever built. The data centres built by Apple, Facebook and Supernap to house their servers have assumed the scale of the sublime. The Switch Supernap Campus in Nevada, for example, contains a building nearly a kilometre long. Like Superstudio's series of Continuous Monuments, these are buildings that begin to curve with the earth's surface. Rem Koolhaas has described them as 'urbanization without people', for they require only a minimal human presence to service and cool thousands of machines. Koolhaas refers to the aesthetic of these places, with their miles of colour-coded pipes and wires and their stack upon stack of servers, as a kind of sublime: 'None of us thought that a building could be this radical: this abstract and codified, uninflected by human need, distant from us and nevertheless produced by us and needed by us.'[9]

In so far as the technological sublime has an aesthetic, this is one of its forms: spaces that are both vast and invisible, too big to take in and yet out of sight. 'Speaking' a language of machinery, they are dehumanized and seem to support no organic life. By contrast, the other form of the technological sublime is overtly organic

Justin McGuirk

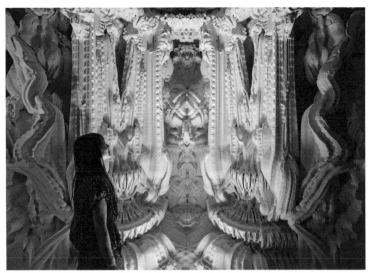

Grotto, a 3D-printed wall surface by Benjamin Dillenburger, which he describes as 'an architecture between chaos and order'

and finds its inspiration in biology. Here, complex 3D printing processes can finally render the complexity of a dragonfly's wing or a plant's cell structure. Those who push the limits of computational, parametric form-making are spawning a digital Gothic that is, in its own way, sublime. Benjamin Dillenburger's 'Digital Grotesque', for example, a 3D-printed surface that resembles a particularly byzantine grotto wall, fetishizes complexity. It is designed to inspire awe and bewilderment, channelling chaos through some computerized natural order. Similarly, Neri Oxman's series of death masks (represented in this book) uses computational complexity and ultra-high-resolution 3D printing to create gothic renditions of heads that mimic intricate natural structures. It is not only in their association with death that they are somehow terrifying; even without those connotations, they stir up something unequivocally dark and strange.

In each case, these are incredible achievements, the very definition of civilization. But civilization – the striving for growth, the mastery of the environment, the endless innovation – has its side effects. Humanity's sheer ingenuity evokes the boundlessness of the sublime. As Bauman so perceptively observes, 'modern civilization owes its morbid (or rather suicidal) potential to the selfsame qualities from which it draws its grandeur and glamour: to its inborn aversion to self-limitation, its inherent transgressiveness and its resentment of, and disrespect for, all and any borders and limits.'

The Two Speeds of the Present
The present feels torn between nostalgia and accelerationism. It is as though we must either slow down – for our sanity, for the sake of our planet – or we must push on to the technological promised land just over the horizon. This speed schizophrenia is, and probably always has been, the taste of the present: slow food, localism and craftsmanship on one hand, and full automation, genetic modification and globalization on the other. This, however, is too simplistic because these positions are not always mutually exclusive.

None of the movements advocating for more sustainable forms of living – whether one considers agriculture or distributed forms of manufacturing – would be able to organize so successfully without the internet and its revolutionary potential for peer-to-peer networking. At the same time, those agitating for a techno-future do not do so because they want to trash the planet. The Ecomodernist Manifesto, for example, asserts that, far from this hippyish notion of getting back in touch with nature, we must intensify human activities such as farming, energy extraction and settlement, and decouple ourselves from nature precisely to protect it.

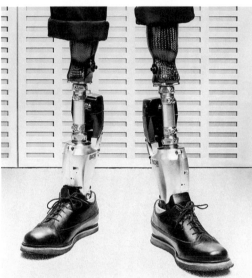

Hugh Herr, head of the Biomechatronics Group at MIT Media Lab, has been developing bionic limbs for amputees.

By the same token, fear and love, which are the two responses to change taken up here, are also not mutually exclusive. They are not opposites but, rather, coexist. As we have seen, that which we love can end up causing us fear. And so there is no divide in the exhibition, or in this book, between those designers dealing in fear and those in love. All of the works represented in this book adopt a more complex, ambiguous attitude to the theme.

We invited designers from diverse disciplines and many corners of the world to address the topic by each creating an installation. Their brief was relatively – perhaps even confusingly – open. In essence, it was to explore an issue that inspires fear and love, and to communicate it in the museum through an immersive experience.

For the purposes of this book, the designers are organized into five sub-themes: network, empathy, periphery, earth and body. These represent a loose framework of issues that are relevant to the way we view design today. Let's begin with the most elemental: *Earth*.

If the term Anthropocene acknowledges anything, it is that we are now designing the planet. This is no metaphor; it is literally true: the term was coined by geologists observing the man-made content of the earth's most recent geological layers, replete with plastics and other fossil-fuel by-products. Playing even more loosely with the term 'design', one might add that we have also designed the weather – though not according to any plan.

The idea that humanity is on the verge of an ecological crisis is not particularly new. Earlier critics of design, such as Victor Papanek and Vance Packard, made the point bluntly and urgently in the 1970s. For Packard, the problem was 'a philosophy of waste', which was the obvious side effect of our fantastic productivity.[10] The need for economic growth demanded that markets must not become saturated with goods and that therefore it was necessary to invent reasons to replace them, such as built-in obsolescence. And while we are wise to this today and have concocted cradle-to-cradle production systems and so-called ethical consumerism, we make so many exceptions as to render these measures useless. Cheap fashion and technological devices are only the most obvious examples. We prefer not to know about the smouldering e-waste dumps, such as Agbogbloshie in Ghana, where many of the two billion mobile phones produced a year go to die. Similarly, our descendants will be incredulous that, back in the early twenty-first century, every time someone wanted a drink of water they would throw away a plastic bottle. Designers are at the forefront of efforts to clean up the Great Pacific Garbage Patch,

Justin McGuirk

'Sterile', a collaboration between Cohen Van Balen and Professor Yamaha Etsuro, 2014. This albino goldfish has been genetically modified not to be able to reproduce.

and they will no doubt pioneer alternatives to plastic packaging. But if we do not act fast, William Gibson's sci-fi tale of an inhabited plastic island in the Pacific may not be so far fetched.[11]

This powerful sense that we are designing, or perverting, nature is equally prevalent at the opposite end of the scale: *Body*. There are innumerable examples of design enhancing the body in the traditionally solutionistic mode. Hugh Herr's bionic limbs, for example, improve life immeasurably for amputees such as himself. But the boundaries between nature and design are becoming increasingly blurred. To stretch design to its limit, one might cite the exquisitely complex realm of sexual identity among the transgender population (such that Facebook notoriously introduced fifty-eight genders to choose from).

As a society we have, arguably, rather conservative views about what the body is and what is 'natural'. Thus, designers and artists court controversy when they use organic cells and DNA as their material. It has been twenty years since scientists grew a mouse with a human ear on its back, and more than a decade since Oron Catts and Ionat Zurr grew a tiny 'victimless leather' jacket in a laboratory, yet these projects remain canonical outliers. Recently, the designers Revital Cohen and Tuur Van Balen worked with a genetic engineer to create an albino goldfish with no reproductive organs – the idea being that, removed from the reproductive cycle, it was now reduced to a product. This notion that we can engineer life has become literal. CRISPR, a kind of bacterial software programme, is now being used to programme DNA – for example, to trigger a healing process or turn off a gene that allows tumours to grow. This realization that even our DNA is malleable, like plastic, gives geneticists some of the qualities of designers.

The distinction between nature and culture has never been less clear. And that extends to our supposedly most *unnatural* products, our machines. The relationship between man and machine is addressed under the theme of *Empathy*. One recurrent motif in the early thinking behind this exhibition was an image of an eagle about to bring down a drone. It was a still from a news video about how Dutch police have been training eagles to hunt unmanned aerial vehicles (UAVs), presumably in anticipation of some kind of infestation. The image is powerful because it defies a deeply rooted logic. For thousands of years, we have built machines to overcome nature; now we have to train nature to control our machines. This epitomizes the strangeness of a two-speed present.

Similarly, though robots were invented to do away with human drudgery, the closer they get to developing human capacities the more we fear them. After a video of a humanoid robot made by

Introduction

An eagle trained by Dutch police to bring down unlicensed aerial vehicles

Boston Dynamics went viral, a spokesman from Google, which owned the company at the time but sold it shortly afterwards, said, 'There's excitement from the tech press, but we're also starting to see some negative threads about it being terrifying, ready to take humans' jobs.' This is the standard fear of automation, that it destroys jobs. At the Davos economic forum in 2016, it was predicted that robots would eliminate five million jobs over the next five years.

And yet, if the socio-economic conditions would let us, we might view this differently. New Babylon, the utopian world conjured by the artist Constant Nieuwenhuys in the 1960s, offered a post-capitalist life free from work. And there are those today who invite such a prospect, arguing for 'fully automated luxury communism' and a universal basic income. So are the machines to be feared or loved? One of the participants of this exhibition, Madeline Gannon, explores that question by attempting to create empathy between the visitors and a giant industrial robot that is ordinarily programmed to do repetitive tasks once undertaken by humans.

In the same way, another theme, *Network*, is as worrying as it is potentially liberating. As we have seen, the revolutionary effects of network culture are transforming design. With open source and distributed manufacturing, it is now possible to imagine a design culture that does not involve mass-production in exploitative conditions, or unsustainable global shipping or big-box retail in petrol-guzzling suburbia. On the other hand, the new, data-driven economy means that we will have to relinquish more and more of our privacy in exchange for basic services. And the drive to connect our domestic products to the internet — to make them 'smart' — threatens to usher in a surveillance culture by stealth. However, rather than dwelling on such orthodox design outputs, Andres Jaque's installation suggests that the network designs behaviour in more fundamental ways. His exploration of locative dating apps, such as Grindr, proposes that such tools are changing our attitudes to relationships, to sex, to our bodies and to the way we now navigate the city.

Finally, it is clear that many of the challenges facing humanity this century lie on the margins of society — in particular, on the edges of the rapidly expanding cities of the global south. The *Periphery* section reflects the idea that design is a necessary component of life in informal or disadvantaged communities. There are currently a billion people on this planet living in slum conditions, and the UN predicts that by 2030 the number will be two billion. Is such a large portion of humanity to be deprived of the infrastructure, housing and products that most Westerners take for

Justin McGuirk

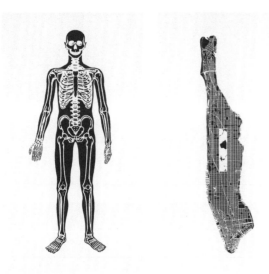
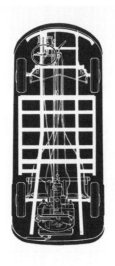

'City Metaphors' by OM Ungers, part of a series of diagrams exhibited in *Man Transforms* at the Cooper Hewitt, Smithsonian Design Museum, New York, in 1976

granted? Those who live in informal communities already display obvious ingenuity, resourcefulness and cooperation, but there will always be features of a comfortable urban life that they cannot provide for themselves: transport networks, sewerage systems, electricity grids and piped water. The discourse of design exists in a predominantly affluent context, but that will have to change if design is to remain relevant to the conditions of scarcity that define the twenty-first century.

A Note on Design Exhibitions
Forty years after *This Is Tomorrow* (1956), the Independent Group's exhibition at the Whitechapel Art Gallery, the artist Richard Hamilton ventured that, since there was nothing particularly futuristic about it, it should really have been called *This Is Today*.[12] That would have been an apt title for this exhibition. While there is much speculation about the future in certain quarters of design, we preferred to try to capture the spirit of the day. *Fear and Love* is resolutely about this strange moment that we call the present. Douglas Coupland, in that catchy way of his, has dubbed it 'the extreme present', which, despite our jealousy, we decided not to borrow.

The first exhibition in the Design Museum, in 1989, was called *Commerce and Culture*. Curated by the director, Stephen Bayley, it displayed everyday consumer goods and argued, essentially, that commerce and culture were no longer separate entities but – through design – had fused. In its curatorial selection, it was in the mode of the *Good Design* exhibitions at the Museum of Modern Art, New York, in the 1950s, and thus confined design to a world of taste and consumer culture. *Fear and Love* is very much not about consumer products, and is at pains to dispense with the idea that we must put products on display to communicate 'design'. And yet we do not present this as progress. In fact, *Fear and Love* is haunted by the ghosts of exhibitions past.

One in particular resonated: *Man Transforms*, which opened the Cooper Hewitt, Smithsonian Design Museum in New York in 1976, exactly forty autumns ago. Its curator, Hans Hollein, sought to break with the already dated notion that museums should be repositories of 'good design', with all the didactic moralism that implied. Indeed, this was one of the first exhibitions to challenge the idea that 'design' meant objects at all. Instead, Hollein presented an attitude – one for which he was already notorious – that 'everything is design'. This was perhaps best illustrated by a long table on which the curators laid every style of bread they could lay their hands on from Manhattan's ethnic bakeries. Everything that humans touch, in other words, is transformed.

Hans Hollein's bread table in *Man Transforms* at the Cooper Hewitt, Smithsonian Design Museum, in 1976

More challenging for the times, arguably, was the use of an artistic mode more common to the art world. Confronted by Arata Isozaki's sculpture of an angel in a cage, or Ettore Sottsass's *Metafore* photo series (in which various string constructions cast shadows), the visitor may well have wondered what these had to do with design. But Hollein's intention was to provoke exactly that question: 'The visitor,' he wrote in the catalogue, 'will both get information but also be brought into a certain mood, a certain receptiveness and willingness to experience, associate, transform, think.'

Fear and Love is very much in this spirit. The idea of commissioning new installations was partly a way to get around the notion that a design exhibition consists of a sequence of objects on plinths. It was of course the riskiest thing we could possibly have done – how much easier to merely select pre-existing works – but also, somehow, the only way to communicate design as an expanded mode: as system, as experience, as a discipline with a stake in emotive issues. It also felt important to make this a multidisciplinary exhibition, to reflect the spectrum of practices that design encompasses. *Fear and Love* brings together a diverse group from around the world – representing architecture, fashion, product design and graphic design – who would not ordinarily share the same gallery.

In many ways, this is an exhibition that could only work as the opening of a new museum. The breadth of the theme allows for the widest possible scope of issues to be addressed. By refusing the specific, we allow a spectrum of voices and attitudes to represent what the new Design Museum can encompass. If we do our jobs well, we will challenge the audience's preconceptions of what design is, and of what a design exhibition is.

1   'The Chapman University Survey on American Fears' (October 2015).
2   Zygmunt Bauman, *Liquid Fear* (Cambridge, 2006).
3   Herbert Read, *New Aspects of British Sculpture* exhibition catalogue (London, 1952).
4   Russell, Andrew and Vinsel, Lee 'Hail the maintainers', *Aeon* (April 7, 2016).
5   Bruce Sterling, *Tomorrow Now: Envisioning the Next 50 Years* (New York, 2002).
6   Lars Spuybroek, *The Sympathy of Things: Ruskin and the Ecology of Design*, (New York, 2011).
7   MoMA's senior curator of architecture and design, Paola Antonelli, has termed objects that lie in a web of complex systems 'knotty objects'.
8   Jesko Fezer and Martin Schmitz, 'Design Is Invisible', in *Lucius Burckhardt Writings. Rethinking Man-made Environments: Politics, Landscape and Design*, eds. Jesko Fezer and Martin Schmitz. (Vienna, 2012).
9   This quote is from an internal AMO document on the increasingly technologized nature of the countryside, part of a research project conducted with students of Harvard's Graduate School of Design.
10 Vance Packard, *The Waste Makers*, (New York, 1960).
11 In *The Peripheral*, (London, 2015), Gibson turns this plastic soup into an island inhabited by 'the patchers'.
12 Interviewed by Hans Ulrich Obrist and Rem Koolhaas at the Serpentine Interview Marathon in 2006.

Network

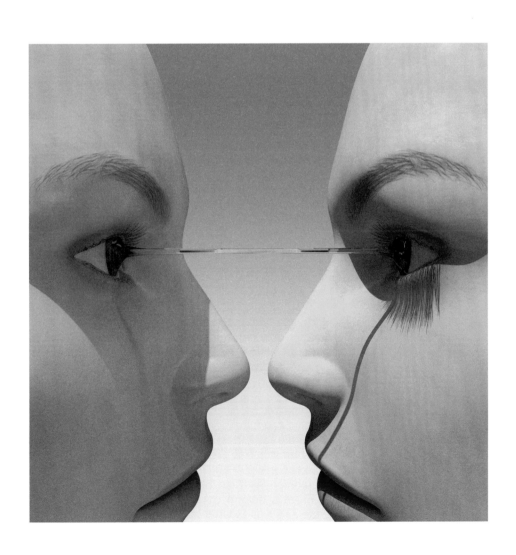

Fear and Love in the Networked Home
Bruce Sterling

Designing networks means creating an architecture of participation. If it is to be a network rather than a mob, then somebody has to design those intangible structures, determining who does what to, or for, whom.

Who looks and who lurks? Who rules and who trolls? Who kisses and who offers the cheek?

Since broadband networks now whip silently in torrents of intangible digits through almost every structure humanity has ever built, we now live in a veritable morass of 'context collapse'. This useful term-of-art, coined by network critic Danah Boyd, describes what happens when the social norms of an unwired society, which existed in our ancient analogue architectures of participation, are promptly blown to hell by the existence of some digital gadget.

Being a novelist, I'll highlight this with an anecdote. Imagine that your father is weeping uncontrollably at your mother's funeral. A funeral is a public event, and attendees, a close group, are fully expected to sympathize with his feelings—in fact, they are there as a body of witnesses to validate his grief. Such is the context, it is proper, it is sombre, it is important. However, your father's red-eyed fit of grief might be recorded by a video mobile service: Vine, Vimeo, Facebook, YouTube—we have lots—and then uploaded to a social network. There, his tears for a lost love might be cruelly transformed into apparent evidence that he is an unmanly and snivelling type. Perhaps, then, he can be portrayed as unfit for public office. Because even though a funeral is public, it's not that kind of public.

What should have been an emotional tribute and an act of familial dignity becomes an act of humiliation. Internet viewers would never rudely barge into your mother's funeral, but a context-free snippet of video can easily become a meme, especially if it benefits some network actor.

In Turin, we have built a place that is a kind of garage laboratory for context collapse. It's called 'Casa Jasmina', and is named after Jasmina Tesanovic, a Serbian feminist and internet activist who is keenly interested in freedom, dignity and Balkan power struggles. It was her idea to try building such a house, and to see if it would really be a 'house'. I participated in the project because I'm a science fiction writer and like to see how people behave in innovative circumstances. Also, because I married Jasmina. We live together.

From a design perspective, the most interesting aspect of Casa Jasmina is what William Gibson might call its 'cyberspace eversion'. Casa Jasmina looks and feels like a house that is experimenting with a network, but it is actually a network experimenting with a house.

The Arduino Diecimila is a microcontroller board launched in 2007, named after the 10,000 (*diecimila*) Arduino boards that had been made by then.

The context of Casa Jasmina is by no means a customary, time-honoured, private and domestic situation. Casa Jasmina arises directly from a Turinese milieu of open source electronics, Maker culture and shareable office space. The architectural envelope for this structure is a huge derelict factory, a former Fiat heavy-metal engine foundry from 1919.

This ultra-sturdy, ferro-cement factory structure was so sternly built that even Allied air bombings couldn't knock it down. Eventually, it collapsed economically, like much of the rest of the European car business, and was abandoned to the elements in the 1970s.

The ruin then sat slowly decaying until an Arduino network of open source zealots showed up, eager for cheap floor space. Arduino is an international company, but basically a digital network of interaction design professors and electronics engineers who took it upon themselves to create a variety of programmable, patent-free internet gadgets, mostly for the student and hobby markets.

Arduino met with surprising success, thanks mostly to buyers from the network-frenzied popular mechanics crowd of the 'Maker Movement'. Since there was plenty of room in their derelict Turinese foundry, the Arduino network also decided to build an MIT-inspired Maker 'Fab Lab', or fabrication laboratory. This shareable hobby shop comes complete with the usual digital Fab Lab regalia of laser cutters, three-dimensional printers, computer-controlled routers, drill presses, hand tools and even a six-axis industrial robot.

The Arduino-based DIY Gamer Kit by Technology Will Save Us allows users of all ages to build and code their own handheld gaming console.

Meanwhile, in the most-nearly habitable part of the building, a chic design office called 'Toolbox Co-working' lofted out the factory and rented office space to local creatives while everybody shared broadband and coffee duties. This made good sense in a property and unemployment crisis. Toolbox Co-working is something close to a conventional business, and represents the architectural 'adult' in a factory full of young, Italian geeks.

Arduino and the Torino Fab Lab are basically social emanations from academia and the hobby world. They have ballooned into near global-institution size, thanks to the ease of global networking. Arduino and Fab Lab people occasionally touch machine tools or electronic devices, but they spend the vast majority of their time networking on the internet. Due to their open source ideology, they tend to shy away from commercial empires such as Google, Apple, Facebook, Amazon and Microsoft, spending their hours on the hackerly likes of GitHub and SourceForge.

It's no secret that Google, Apple, Facebook, Amazon and Microsoft are all keen to design an 'internet-of-things' home.

Bruce Sterling

Project Loon is a research venture developed by Google to provide the internet to the two-thirds of the world's population that don't yet have access to it.

Arduino, the Fab Lab and the Maker Movement would also like to be involved in some internet-of-things form of domesticity. However, they want it designed to suit their shareable, non-patented, hobby-centric, only vaguely commercial version of the internet – the kind where small clusters of geek zealots cheerily make their own things.

Casa Jasmina is therefore a propaganda of the deed – it is the product of Italian social networks that decided that since they could 'make' things, they could make a house.

There is absolutely no question that Google, Apple, Facebook, Amazon and Microsoft all have access to vastly better industrial design than Arduino. However, their operational difficulty is that they would like to dominate their internet of things in much the way that they have attempted to dominate the internet. They can't simply pitch in pell-mell, in a network-society 'barn raising' as Arduino did with Casa Jasmina. Their interests are too large, and their architecture of participation is too big.

Google, for instance, would like to search, catalogue and organize the internet of things by putting it on their Android platform, along with Google cars, mobile robots, aerial Google Loon balloons and any prestige moon shots from their own ecosystem.

Apple, as is their custom, aim for a boutique, high-profit-margin internet of things, where they trade high price for ease of use, consistent design, relative security and sleek Jony Ive touchpoints for every possible interface.

Facebook, being a social network, would socialize people in homes, with 'Facebook M' as their deep-learning, always-on, always-listening major-domo.

Amazon sell things, so they would attach selling buttons to as many internet-of-things commodities as they could – while Amazon Alexa, the verbal interface posing as a music speaker, could fetch and ship anything you express a desire to have.

Microsoft, if they can manage it, will use their huge installed base in business and government to come up with the mainstream, 'pinstriped' version of what everybody else is doing.

Such are the design problems of the network majors, and they are quite severe. Even Hitachi, Xiaomi and Samsung would quite like a domestic internet-of-things package, but their vast scale and complex arrangements with allies, competitors and customers strongly militate against just tossing an internet-of-things house package off the back of a truck.

They would love to do it, but it's an epic and fearsome effort – and that's just how it is. Microsoft, Amazon, Facebook, Apple and Google happen to be the dominant enterprises of the decade,

Network

In 2015, Amazon launched the Dash Button, designed to deliver preset products – in this case, detergent – to your door at the push of a button.

and it's quite natural that they would try to use the methods that brought them great success in cyberspace to the rest of the physical landscape.

There are issues of context collapse in this that can't be avoided or papered over, even with the best design efforts. The majors fear the humiliation, the brand damage, of moving too precipitously into social arenas where it's practically impossible to get it right. Every 'collapse in context' is actually a clash of contexts. These contexts have tender membranes in order to surround and contain different aspects of living.

To return to our example of love and grief: if your blundering cousin takes his Apple smartphone to your mother's funeral, it's not because he deliberately meant to insult you in a ghoulish fashion. On the contrary, he did that because he literally always has his Apple smartphone handy – because, according to Apple, the average iPhone gets unlocked eighty times a day.

His phone is the first thing he touches in the morning and the last thing he touches at night. He collapsed the context because his own context is to take a selfie whenever anything memorable happens. Your mother getting buried was memorable to him, so when you step in to remark, 'Hey, you are not supposed to selfie your aunt's open casket,' that contextual boundary assertion is something of an act of micro-aggression that dents his self-esteem.

He might even assert that time is on his side, that mobile phones used to be rude even in streets and restaurants, and now they're not even rude in some cinemas, and that therefore it's really you who rudely rent the context.

At Casa Jasmina, we spend rather a lot of time on design issues of contextuality, or what they used to call privacy issues – who gets to look at whom, when. But from the first day, we've done this with mobiles in our hands. These mobiles, which run on Apple iPhone OS and Google Android platforms, are vastly more powerful and capable than any prototype or hobby object we've built or brought into Casa Jasmina.

We're therefore rather like gourmands discussing barbecue sauce next to a slaughterhouse – not that this is a counsel of despair, or anything! It is realism to accept the fact that the context is already ripped to shreds by billions of active smartphones planetwide. This keeps us from imagining ourselves in some analogue, dropout idyll where we get to set all the parameters ourselves.

It's customary to close an act of technology assessment, such as this one, by asking plaintively if anything can save us. Not really. We don't want to be saved from 'surveillance'. Surveillance is a politicized subset of media practice generally, and we are

Opendesk is a platform for distributed furniture manufacturing. Anyone can download or adapt designs released under Creative Commons licences, eliminating shipping costs in favour of local fabrication.

Casa Jasmina is a laboratory for experiments in home automation and the 'internet of things', located in an abandoned industrial building in Turin, Italy. It was established by Arduino co-founder Massimo Banzi and author Bruce Sterling.

by far the most mediated culture ever. We love surveillance as much as we detest it; we merely rename it, and give it some softer label – 'transparency', 'security', 'awareness', 'convenience', 'smartness' – whenever it seems to give us our desires.

It's also a mistake to think that open source is helpless in the paralytic grip of the major commercial players. They are the largest and best-capitalized companies on earth presently, but just as bewildered as everybody else. The major players rather enjoy having open source activists around – like guys with an air force who befriend a tribal militia.

Open source is still toxic to standard capitalism – or even 'cancerous', as Microsoft used to put it, because it has become a method to give away the other guy's revenue stream.

If you can simply give away what a commercial rival gets money for doing, then you have stripped them of capital and revenue without having to compete with them directly. It's become subtle yet effective, like some sly act of passive-aggression. To open a source is not a utopian matter of all information being free for everybody; on the contrary, in the emerging architecture of participation in an internet of things, the power player aspires to the position of 'Information *About You* Wants to Be Free *to Me*.'

When a power player forces surveillance on an unwilling party, it's rarely called 'surveillance' by the watcher. Instead, it becomes 'transparency', or 'security', or 'public safety', or 'accountability' or some other public virtue. It's only when it's done to me, and I don't approve, that it becomes sneaking, spying, stalking, doxxing, trolling, cyberwar, industrial espionage, leaking or similar pejoratives for the pain of context collapse.

Surveillance and privacy are not design absolutes like an on-and-off switch; they are political positions in an architecture of participation. If I watch over you constantly and you are a two-year-old girl, that is the gaze of concern and loving care; if you are a twenty-two-year-old woman, that is voyeurism. That's why cot cameras are generally beloved and street cameras tend towards the creepy except in, say, London.

Nobody would argue that an infant's cot is an Orwellian environment. Technically, yes, it can be, but emotionally, no. Therefore, we're exceedingly keen to invent ingenious methods for monitoring infants: microphones, motion sensors, video cameras, medical devices. Babies never resent that invasion of their privacy: they're too absorbed in the heroic effort of lifting their heads and turning over. However, every device that's pioneered in a nursery has some technical dual-use in prisons and emigration zones. We feel differently about it, but as hardware, it's all the same.

The Drone Aviary by Superflux is a speculative investigation of the social, political and cultural implications of drone technology as it enters civil space.

The elderly need attention. They die from too much privacy. What they desire is dignity. There is far more dignity in surveillance by impartial machines than there is in the grim corral of some elder-care hostel. This implies that the elderly will choose independence as long as they can, while forfeiting more and more control over daily life to algorithms, sensors and mechanisms.

We're busily creating a world where surveillance rules unquestioned over both youth and decline. 'Privacy' becomes a radically narrowed condition, deserved only by vigilant and responsible adults.

There are odder, smaller consequences to the saturation of surveillance technologies. Surveillance can be auto-eroticized; it can be turned on the self. This would be the 'Instrumented Self', that modern hobby-cult with stark, medical overtones.

Some technically minded early adopters do take a keen interest in exploring aspects of their own metabolism. To 'know thyself' is an old philosophical injunction. There's plenty revealed by novel imaging technologies that was formerly inaccessible. Nowadays, one can parse and crack one's own DNA, study exercise and sleeping patterns, blood counts for various substances, diet, urinalysis, and even that teeming microbe biome in the gastrointestinal tract which is rather fetid and malodorous but as little-known as the rainforests of the Amazon.

To date, this new school of self-surveillance remains a hypo-chondriacal hobby because there's little evidence that it actually improves your health. But it might. If it did prove to be of practical benefit, you could expect this private, introverted and even spiritual practice to turn aggressively evangelical.

The politics of self-instrumentation would shift radically, as surveillance so commonly does. Instrumented Mum, bound by love and duty, would medically surveil the kids. Wife and Husband would lash out with proof of the spouse's irritating vices of smoking and overeating. Poor Grandpa, already beset with his aches and pains, would clank with surveillance devices while nettled with blood-test pinpricks. Big Brother would come home for a nap.

In all these cases, the design of the hardware tends to uniformity for engineering reasons; all cameras tend to a small, half-hidden condition of what used to be expensive spy-cameras. Obviously Google and Facebook have fantastic resources, but one of the reasons they don't build fully branded Google and Facebook homes is that they're afraid that a rival might move into one. If an Apple executive can't live in an Amazon home for fear of surveillance, the gloves are off for the internet of things—they'll all be revealed as surveillance silos, and an 'arms race' might break out.

The Dropcam, subsequently bought by Nest and rebranded the Nest Cam, is a miniature indoor security camera that can monitor burglars or babies.

Bruce Sterling

Echo was introduced by Amazon in 2014 as a domestic, voice-enabled device designed to provide real-time information and control a wide number of 'smart' home devices.

I don't expect these social issues to be adroitly designed away; that would be like attempting to design a camera that can't possibly take a picture of a mother in a casket. Such a feat is not entirely impossible, but it requires a level of control of technology like that of old-fashioned photocopiers, which had a built-in inability to scan and copy American dollars. It's become much easier to mess with the paper than to control electronics, so contemporary US paper currency looks as absurd as a circus poster and would have caused my American ancestors to break out laughing. Context collapse has an element of absurdity, of farce; it's too much to think that we can purge ourselves of that aspect of the human condition.

What really interests me about Casa Jasmina – and why I consider it, in its own modest way, a successful intervention – is that people do treat it as a house. More to the point, they can't seem to help that. Casa Jasmina is not a house, it is actually a second-storey set of industrial offices which are merely furnished and painted as a 'house'.

No actual family has ever lived in the 'house', and although it has a dedicated 'children's room', the kids in Casa Jasmina are entirely fictitious. After all, the house is upstairs from a Fab Lab full of hazardous saws, lasers, hammers and soldering irons. So any tot wandering out the front door could easily come to harm; even a kitten or puppy would be a risk.

And yet, the participants in Casa Jasmina behave as if it's a house. When they enter the front door of the place – it only has one door – they are somehow overcome by the power of the change of context.

Casa Jasmina has rather eccentric furniture – most of it built to digital plans, from plywood, with digitized saws and drills – but since it smells like coffee and Italian food and there are beds, chairs and artwork, it's perceived and treated as a house.

People change their deportment in it, even if their workplace is ten steps away. Their body language changes, and the topics of conversation move. I wouldn't even claim that they stop 'working', but their work, instead of being a set of paid tasks carried out, becomes part of the general work of socialization.

A Fab Lab has Maker equipment, while a Maker house has a maker culture. People actually go to Casa Jasmina because they enjoy its acculturation.

A Fab Lab is allegedly democratic because it aims to struggle to lower the barriers of access to technology, but a Fab Lab – with its racket, industrial smells and air of hard-won technical mastery – is actually quite intimidating. Also, the zealots in a Fab Lab are busy

Most of the furniture at Casa Jasmina has been designed in partnership with Opendesk, the platform for open-source furniture.

with their own projects: I've seen them remain emotionally focused even when a mayor or an astronaut walks by.

A house, by contrast, is more gracious than that. It has design affordances that no 'machine-for-living' can give. This is so even though Casa Jasmina was never an authentic home, and has always had aspects that could only belong in a lab or a showroom: bare wires, half-disassembled Arduino gizmos, tables cut from Foamcore, and so on. However, just the least little set of design gestures – a laden flower vase, some curtains, background music, a bookshelf, cozy towels – somehow, that is enough to change the architecture of participation. It slams a new context into being, with, really, a crushing force.

And although I know all this, and I can write it, I myself can't help it. Whenever I'm in Casa Jasmina, I'm in a fictional house – and yet, I'm a real host.

Andrés Jaque /
Office for Political Innovation
Intimate Strangers

Andrés Jaque is the founder of Andrés Jaque Architects and the Office for Political Innovation. He has developed a series of architectural experiments intended to explore design from a political perspective, including *IKEA Disobedients* (2011), which was the first architectural performance ever included in the collection of MoMA, New York, and *Superpowers of Ten* (2015), a performance based on the narrative and ideas of Charles and Ray Eames's 1977 film *Powers of Ten*. He is professor of Advanced Architectural Design at the Columbia University Graduate School of Architecture, Planning and Preservation, and visiting professor at Princeton University School of Architecture.

COSMO, MoMA PS1, New York, 2015

Superpowers of Ten, Lisbon Architecture Triennale, 'Close, Closer', Lisbon, Portugal, 2013

Rolling House for the Rolling Society, prototype of a shared European home, Construmat, Barcelona, 2009

Phantom: Mies as Rendered Society, Mies van der Rohe Pavilion, Barcelona, 2012

At the end of the twentieth century, people were predicting a future in which physical proximity would no longer be necessary. Instead, we would have virtual relationships. Such predictions turned out to be unfounded. The launch of 3G portable devices equipped with global positioning (GPS) in 2008, followed by locative geosocial media (LGM) in 2009, made it easier than ever for people to come to together. In just eight years, the design of location-based, real-time dating (LRD), proximity-based people discovery (PBPD), Facebook's Nearby Friends and other 'hook-up' apps have not only transformed the way we find friendship, love and sex, but also attitudes to our cities and even our bodies. Badoo, Blender, Blued, Down, Glimpse, Grindr, happn, Hinge, Jack'd, JSwipe, Manhunt, Pure, SCRUFF, Tinder – together they amount to an alternative form of urbanism fueled by sex and love. These overlapping networks have been specifically developed to detach sex from familiarity, or to present sex as a perpetually available infrastructure that allows strangers to become intimate.

Location is back, but not in the same way as before. In PBPD, presence is not exact but coarse-grained. It is not a spot on a map but an estimation of the time it would take to meet. Available user profiles are no longer determined by fixed distances but by changing densities. In rural areas, hundreds of kilometres separate potential lovers; in cities and airport hotels, it might be a matter of metres. Location is no longer an identity but a behaviour – it is not based on 'belonging to a place' but on the opportunism of where you happen to be. Profiles are not meant to be transparent representations of users' bodies or minds ('they all lie' is a common refrain), but to sexualize members so that their path to intercourse can be *smoothed*. If precision, permanence and trustworthiness were once the foundations of urban relationships, they are now approximation, promiscuity and self-pornification.

Locative love is not forever, it is not for sweethearts, it is not about finding one's 'other half'. With locative love, digital ubiquity has become ubiquitous sex. Meanwhile, anonymity and identity fabrication have become tools of mutual trust. Tinder alone operates in more countries than the United Nations. Together with Badoo and Grindr, these platforms have mobilized a mass of users almost equivalent to the entire population of the US. Through locative love, urbanites have reinvented themselves as those who develop their intimacy with strangers.

Launched in 2009 by Nearby Buddy Finder, and majority-owned by Beijing Kunlun Tech, Grindr was the first gay-men-oriented LGM. There are more than one million active Grindr users at any time. Yet twenty per cent of the company's servers are located in countries where gay sex is banned. It has been seen as a space for LGBT emancipation, providing access to sex to a global population of gay men, of which no less than eleven per cent remain closeted. An endless stream of single-men profiles is available for users to check, by dragging their fingers across sexy photographs behind the potassium-coated ion-strengthened glass of their smartphones. Grindr has helped to normalize gayness. It has become a place for gay celebrities to be seen, streaming media for JW Anderson's 2016 summer menswear show, a place for *PAPER* magazine to recruit models. Grindr has also been seen as an alternative queer space in the age of same-sex marriage. The app has been criticized for its contribution to transforming gay scenes from spaces of gender activism into contexts of healthy looking individuality and one-to-one intercourse, shifting gay societies from being spaces of collective activism to networks of comfortable lifestyle consumption.

Grindr is urban, but it is not a city. It is not fixed to a piece of land but distributed in unstable constellations. Bodies, mirrors, cellphones, servers, satellites, clothes, skins, backgrounds, software, interfaces … they all participate in the making of a collective neural system, unapologetically jumping from one city to another, and into the countryside. Not just accommodated by the urban, Grindr has become a kind of urbanism in its own right. It is both super-immaterial and super-material. It is a network of constantly moving parts, linked by desire. The setting is permanently active, constantly being produced: by updating profiles, by dragging one profile to the next one, by disappearing from one person's screen to become available on another's. If Richard Buckminster Fuller dreamt of a world of omnidirectional connectivity in the air, Grindr is it. It is an urban enactment in which LGBT realities are made in online and offline realms, where proximity, intimacy, profiling and the mathematics of sex are experienced and disputed. Urban tribes are defined and empowered, and racial or bodily features ('no blacks', 'no fems', 'no fat') become reasons for rejection. Isolated gay men, living in countries where homosexual practices are banned and punished, gain access to an alternative space for interaction. Intolerant governments can also use Grindr to track, harass and arrest gay men. But at a time when many Western cities are being sanitized through gentrification, locative sex has become an urbanism in which emancipation, empowerment, connection, rejection, crime – love and fear – are brought together.

'Intimate Strangers' argues that proximity-based people discovery (PBPD) – 'hook up' software – is one of the most significant designs of the past decade. Our proposal is not meant to solve problems but to reconstruct the way human relationships happen. The multimedia installation is based on original research and independent fieldwork carried out in Grindr's headquarters in West Hollywood, and relies on an ethnography of Grindr networks in different cities around the world. The installation offers visitors the opportunity to enter Grindr interactions and follow the way it transforms its users' relationships with their bodies, with individuals and with the collective. Through six recreated historical episodes, visitors will experience some of the risks and possibilities of Grindr played to their limits.

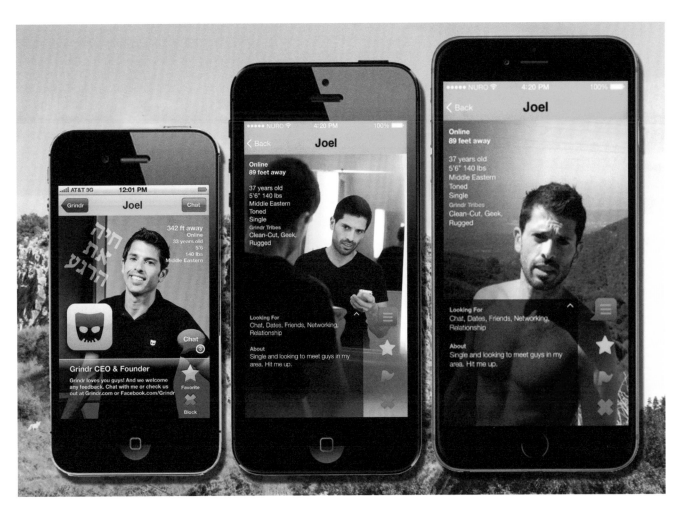

The dating app Grindr allows you to edit your profile with your picture, physical description – such as age, height, body type and relationship status – and your interests. This is the profile for Joel Simkhai, founder and CEO of Grindr.

Most dating apps – including Grindr, Tinder and happn – are based on GPS location systems that enable users to connect with other people nearby. Since these apps use proximity to locate partners, some users hack their locations to access more profiles.

Andrés Jaque / Office for Political Innovation

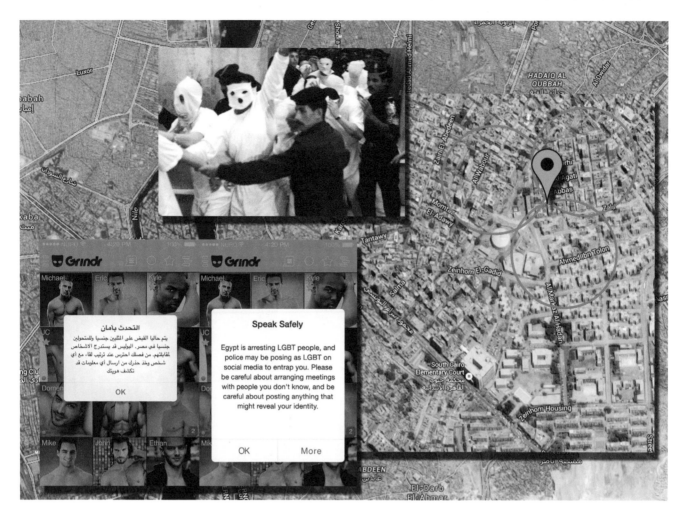

On 12 October 2013, fourteen suspects were arrested after being caught 'in the act of homosexuality' inside a health spa in the poor neighbourhood of al-Marg, northeast of Cairo. Whereas Grindr has become a means for LGBT empowerment, its GPS location basis has also been used in countries where public homosexuality is banned to track, harass and arrest Grindr users.

Dating apps' interfaces have developed in parallel with the evolution of cell phones and interaction features in order to create a more intuitive user experience. Grindr's user interface (*left*) works across multiple devices and offers a wall of profiles at a glance.

Stills from William Mean's documentary *The Grindr Project* (2013). This short film explores, through a series of interviews with various Grindr users, the taboos and controversies around the use of this app. In the film, the interviewees are asked about how this app has influenced the way gays and bisexuals interact in and outside the online platform.

Andrés Jaque / Office for Political Innovation

Andrés Jaque in conversation with Gonzalo Herrero

GH AJ

Your architecture practice is called
the Office for Political Innovation.
How do you think architecture and
politics relate to each other today?

Architecture is always political because
it brings conflicting entities together.
In our office, we are not interested in
political rhetoric or party politics but in
the way our material world is constructed
by politics. We're interested in how
politics is built by daily actions bringing
together different scales, times and
natures. This notion of politics makes
architecture relevant, and reveals
the role it plays in reinventing the social.
We don't focus on the production
of objects but on the way things interact
with each other, and the networks and
layers that creates.

Is this shift leading to a rupture
between applied and theoretical
designers?

Architecture is no longer about finding
solutions – it's about redefining problems
and finding ways to operate in society.
An office like ours can't find an established critical ground to operate in, so we
need to keep producing it. This means
we need to produce research, and find
partners to develop unsolicited projects.
In the broad picture of architectural
practices, there is a clear distinction
between those who claim to be critical
and those who don't want to waste
energy on anything except getting more
commissions. We are moving to a time
in which theories are not important.
What is important is the way we make
everyday practices critical ones.
Received wisdom is being very much
challenged by intelligence-in-the-making.
In other words, knowledge is created
through action. That means that architecture can produce knowledge and
challenge stereotypes. Of course, a lot
of this intelligence comes with the way
technology is embedded in our daily
lives. But we don't have access to the
way that technology is scripted, so
we have to make the context react to
our actions.

GH AJ

How do you approach this in
your practice?

At the Office for Political Innovation, we
have dedicated a lot of effort to examining
fragments of daily life and to questioning
the way they are constructed through
design. It also implies exploring alternative formats for design – like, for instance,
the use of the re-enactment as a design
tool, as we did in the project 'Superpowers
of Ten'. There, we re-enacted a version
of the Eames's Powers of Ten to bring in
the politics that was hidden between the
frames of their original film.

Did you see yourself practising
architecture in this way when you
were a student?

I never imagined myself following the
route that other people were taking:
working in a well-known office, becoming a younger version of the kind of
architect the office was based on,
winning competitions, etc. As a student
at architecture school, I was already
writing for newspapers, working on
research projects in the political sciences and having conversations with people
who saw architecture from the perspective of sociology, ecological politics, or
science and technology. I never pictured
myself following a master. Back when
I was a student, Madrid was a very lively
city, one that came alive at night.
The night-time was much richer than
my daytime life at school. Madrid's
nightlife was a bigger influence on my
current work than architecture school.

Do you think our rapidly changing
world is causing a shift in
our understanding of design?

Design is changing. It's not just that we
inhabit a world that is totally designed
– there is no longer such a thing as
nature – but also that we can only inhabit
the world by participating in its permanent reinvention. What Hans Hollein said
of architecture in 1968 now applies to

design: 'everything is design'.
The moment we wake up in the morning, we start posting online and responding to messages on our phones. Our lives are becoming a design activity. We inhabit a moment in which living means designing and so 'design' is no longer delegated to 'designers'. It is expanding into something that needs to be practised at every moment and by everyone. This is not limited to people but also applies to machines. They are designing themselves, and are starting to become autonomous in the way they shape our existence. This kind of exponential evolution is exciting but also causes a lot of uncertainty – I don't think we are ready for this.

How have you represented this in your installation for *Fear and Love*?

Love and sex are often perceived as sources of security, pleasure and relief from the anxieties of daily life. This idea, however, has become obsolete. The way sex tends to be performed today, in particular through the use of locative social media, is overexposing us to uncertainty in the way we experience sex and affection. The acceleration of sexual satisfaction and love comes with a daily cost in risk and disappointment. The interaction of online and offline spaces where the excitement of intimacy with strangers can occur is in itself a new form of urbanism – a new way of inhabiting the city that produces new kinds of citizens and civic manners. Old forecasts about the future of cities predicted that digital technologies would make location unimportant. Dating apps, such as Tinder and Grindr, show that location is in fact more significant now than ever, but not as a source of familiarity but the other way around. The digital proximity given by these apps is the scenario where we become intimately closer with strangers.

And how is this reflected in architecture and design?

Some of our previous projects, such as The Rolling House for the Rolling Society, Sales Oddity or Cosmo are actually trying to explore how design could operate in these digital locative regimes. The most important thing that's happening is that design is starting to be socially distributed. It's something that is not only happening or being practised by certain actors in the network, but is something that the whole system is producing. This forces architects and designers to rethink the way they work, and the way their work is relevant.

How is this represented in the exhibition?

In this project, we want to create an installation to communicate the situation created by locative geosocial dating apps. This project doesn't try to create a new reality, but to work as a visualizer of an actual, daily social reality. Perhaps it could help design practitioners understand the way they can contribute, or at least the way they are affected by something like locative dating media.

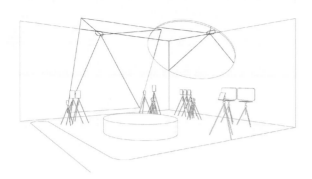

Andrés Jaque's and the Office for Political Innovation's installation for *Fear and Love* proposes a multi-screen display analysing location-based apps at different scales—from identity definition with profile design to the impact on social interaction, both online and face-to-face, and data visualization on an urban map in different times and at landmark events, such as the 2012 London Olympics.

Andrés Jaque / Office for Political Innovation

In 2012, 'Block' was reported as the most used Grindr command. It instigated the development of a number of independent apps with which Grindr users hacked the platform.

In 2015, screenshots of Reverend Matthew Makela's private messages and pictures on Grindr caused controversy when they were published alongside his previous public statements criticizing the LGBT community. The case revealed the discrepancy between some users' public profiles and their private—though not private enough—personas.

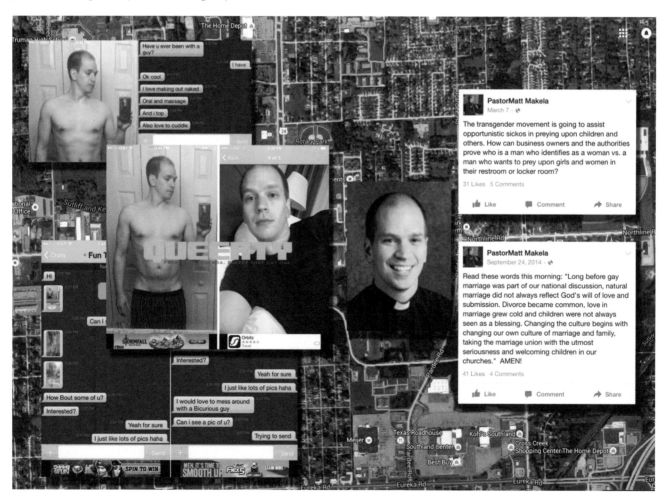

Dating apps are quickly expanding their business market into lifestyle consumer platforms and creating partnerships with fashion brands, event companies and media. In early 2016, London fashion brand JW Anderson partnered with Grindr to live-stream their Spring/Summer 2016 collection show, and in summer that year Grindr debuted its own twenty-nine-piece menswear line titled 'The Varsity Collection'.

OMA
The Pan-European
Living Room

OMA / AMO is an international practice, co-founded by Rem Koolhaas in 1975. Where OMA operates within the traditional boundaries of architecture and urbanism, AMO, a research and design studio, applies architectural thinking to domains beyond. In 2004, AMO designed a coloured 'barcode' flag, combining the flags of all EU member states.

Tools For Life furniture range for Knoll at the Salone del Mobile, Milan, 2013

Holland Green residential development on the Design Museum site, London, 2016

Elements of Architecture, exhibition, 14th Architecture Biennale, Venice, 2014

CCTV (China Central Television) Headquarters, Beijing, 2012

We invented the EU barcode some fifteen years ago: an alternative, colourful symbol for the European Union. A symbol of optimism. The EU could be fun – that was the idea.

At the time such optimism seemed warranted, but in 2016 that spirit seems hard to maintain. This summer, Britain decided to 'jump ship', sparking similar discussions in the Netherlands, France and Austria as to whether the interest of individual nations would not be better served when 'free' to pursue their individual course, unimpeded by interference from Brussels. That national sovereignty needs to be preserved and restored to its former absolute state seems to be the sentiment of many, and not just Britain.

This installation tells a different story. It shows a simple living room: the type you could find in any European home, including Britain. The everyday objects in the room – table, chairs, sofa – have their origins in various European countries. In total, there are twenty-eight items – one from each EU member state – which together constitute the room's interior, making it a showroom of European design and therefore also, inadvertently, of European collaboration.

Vertical blinds, reflecting the colours of the EU barcode, control the amount of light and ensure privacy. Invented and patented in the US in the 1950s (around the same time the European project started), vertical blinds have been applied across Europe as one of the cheapest and most effective ways of covering windows and screening sunlight. Featured in interiors from Sweden to Italy, from Ireland to Greece, vertical blinds have become the silent witnesses of an emerging European unity.

The system isn't perfect: the connection between the slat and the pivoting head, from which the slat hangs on to the mechanism, is fragile and often breaks or disconnects. In this particular room, it is the slat that carries the colours of the Union Jack that has broken off, leaving an opening through which we see the daunting remnants of Europe's historic past.

In the context of overheated debates, bloated anti-European rhetoric and the media frenzy that follows, this simple room serves as understated evidence that there is a European project no matter what, which continues despite recent setbacks. European integration is a fact of life, which transcends short-term performance indicators and constitutes an essential vehicle that gives us our security, comfort and all the other wonderful certainties we tend to take for granted.

In a world where the most pressing issues inevitably exceed the size of nations, interdependence between nations is a given. 'Brexit' does nothing to change that. More than just a political phenomenon, Europe is a form of modernization – or, rather, a chance for the political sphere to catch up with modernization. Interdependence between nations is a direct result of scientific and technological progress, which, once unleashed, cannot be reversed. When problems escalate, so must inevitably the arena in which they are addressed. An institution like the EU is born out of the knowledge that in the face of the bigger issues we are *all* minorities. Countries in Europe have a choice: they can either realize or ignore the fact that they are small. Yet small they all are, including Britain.

The United Kingdom is a modern nation, the origin of the Industrial Revolution, former centre of a global empire and, largely as a consequence, currently home to a global community. More than any other European country, Britain has been affected by other cultures. A retreat within its own borders is not only anti-European or anti-modern, but ultimately un-British. This simple living room offers ample proof of that.

The installation will consist of the following components:

The Barcode
An alternative symbol for the EU: a chromatic line up of all colours of all European flags, running from west to east. The barcode can be expanded as more countries join the European Union, or – though this was not anticipated at the time – it can be reduced if a member state decides to leave. Although it was never proposed that the barcode replace the twelve-star European flag, it has often been touted as such – particularly by the British press. Currently, the barcode enjoys wide exposure as a popular symbol and it generously advertises a number of European products and ideas. The barcode was featured on the cover of a number of international newspapers when the EU was awarded the Nobel Peace Prize in 2013.

The Blinds
In 1950, Edward and Frederick Bopp from Kansas City, Missouri invent and patent the vertical blind under the company name 'Sun Vertical'. Similarly to venetian blinds, vertical blinds are a series of slats that can be made from a variety of materials, but instead of being horizontal these blinds hang vertically from a horizontal track system. Slats can be rotated by a shaft in the overhead rail housing, which runs through independent geared carriers that convert twisting of the rail to a rotation of each individual slat, in synchrony.

The Interior
The interior is that of a typical European living room. The everyday items in the room – twenty-eight in total, one from each EU country – make this simple living room into a showroom of European design. The furniture is Europe, emphasizing Europe's fundamental commitment to modernity. Evidence that, despite the UK's recent political choice, the process of Europe's cultural integration continues, with or against the odds. Our most intimate daily environment constitutes the most eloquent example of Europe's collaboration.

'Europe in Reverse' Video
A short video to the sound of a ticking clock. The clock ticks backwards through the years until 1933, when the Nazis took control of Germany. The video painfully makes clear that not *that* long ago Europe was a continent in shambles. Europe's achievements are surprisingly recent, and have accumulated at a fast pace. Unfortunately, the current anti-European momentum suggests that they could unravel at a fast pace too. If you think Europe is all about bureaucracy, think again!

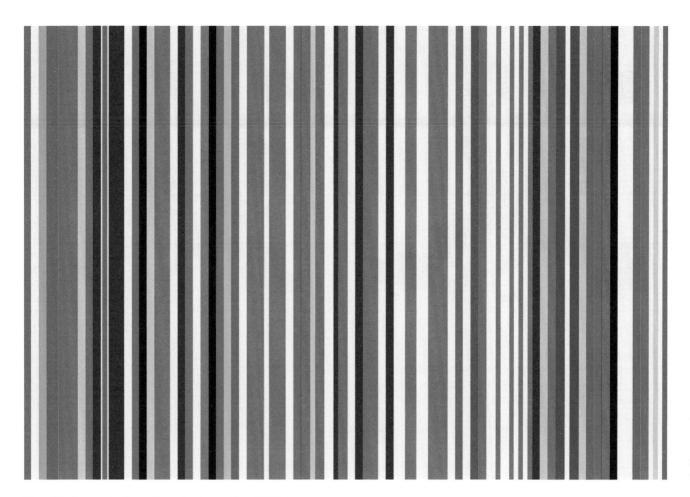

The EU barcode flag–first designed by OMA in 2004 and here updated with its most recent member, Croatia–depicts Europe as the sum of its members' cultural identities.

The iconography of the European Union reduced
the continent to 'Blueurope'. Instead of such
homogeneity, OMA proposed that the iconography
should emphasize cultural and regional diversity.

Reinier de Graaf and Samir Bantal in conversation with Justin McGuirk

JM   RDG   SB

Your project takes up the spirit of OMA's Elements exhibition for the 2014 Venice Biennale of Architecture, in which you explored the basic elements of architecture. In this case you've taken a ubiquitous product—a vertical blind—and politicized it.

Yes, in response to 'Brexit' we propose to create a pan-European living room with one wall made of vertical blinds that recreate OMA's barcode flag for the European Union. It turns out that the vertical blind was another invention of the 1950s, just as the European Union was, so they are contemporaries. Except that, where the blinds were invented to protect us from light and prying eyes, here the European version protects us against—or in this case reveals glimpses of—the past horrors of a disunited Europe.

So the blinds are a metaphorical device?

Absolutely. It's a mechanism that aligns all these vertical elements that are separate and yet don't function separately. So the blinds are a metaphor that nothing functions on its own.

And the living room you propose is a cocktail of European interior design that is both generic and idealistic.

The living room is a kind of prototype of European collaboration, made up of furniture, carpets and objects from the twenty-eight member states. And the point is that any living room you see anywhere in Europe is a product of that integration. So the integration is there whether you 'Brexit' or not. It's just going to make life more difficult for yourselves.

Stop rubbing it in! But elaborate on how this relates to fear and love.

The whole theme of fear and love has taken shape under our very eyes in the evening news. The relationship between Britain and Europe—if ever there was an epitome of the theme fear and love, it's that relationship. So that's also what this installation visualizes: the fear and love in the political and media domain, which will profoundly affect Britain for some time to come.

And how does this situation affect you as architects? How do you see your role in all of this?

Our role in this is, first of all, to express utter regret. But we have had a role in this. As an architect, you normally steer clear of choosing political sides because sides change all the time and it's bad for business to express political views. That's why a lot of

contemporary architects are remarkably unpolitical.
We chose, in 2004, to express our support for the
European Union, which isn't supported by everyone.
That was, in a way, taking political sides as a business.
In fact, the barcode flag is one of our best-known
products, better known than many of our buildings.
Ten years later, you might wonder how smart that was.
We asked ourselves, 'Would we do it again?' And
the answer was, 'Absolutely', because short-term
performance indicators don't affect your support for
things. It shows the extent to which a firm like ours
can be political.

To get these twenty-eight pieces of furniture, we
have to approach numerous companies to lend us
the pieces – so it relies on a coalition of European
manufacturers, committing to be part of a
political statement.

It also sends the message that national sovereignty
is a myth. I mean, look at our business, look at your
business, look at the average living room – the
contents are from everywhere. National sovereignty
has long been a myth, and it's in the name of a myth
that currently political choices are being swayed.
In a subtle way, it's the living room that exposes the
big lie. Through little things like the vase of flowers
on the table, the lamp, the rocking chair or whatever,
ordinary things become momentarily a form
of propaganda – they come clean about the truth.

We could probably represent every country with
an object from Ikea, viewing this ideal of European
collaboration entirely through the eyes of a Swedish
multinational. Does that pervert the message?

But this is not about a single company or country
as narrator. Ikea has capitalized on the diversity of
Europe, but at the same time Ikea designs are more
or less supposed to tell the Swedish story. Our room
represents a more complex condition. The irony
is that even those against Europe live in a European
composition, made possible by EU trade deals.

Is 'Europe' a design project?

It is one of the greatest design projects ever made,
a brave effort to define what unites countries rather
than divides them. And this optimism was well
represented in post-war European design culture.
One could say that the birth of Europe coincided with
the birth of European Design. But the idea of national
design cultures – Italian, Danish or British – has
been replaced by one of international collaboration.
Dutch or French designers work with Italian or
Swedish manufacturers in a globalized marketplace.

And is there a piece of British design in the room?

Of course. Maybe something broken. A tea set, just to
underline the stereotype, with a sticker saying 'SOLD'.

A symbol of unification and interdependence, the barcode flag forms the backdrop to the EU exhibition in Brussels and Vienna (*left*).

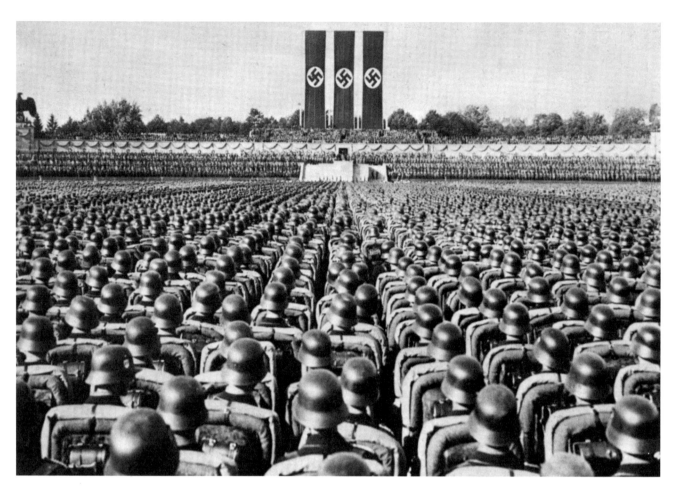

The horrors of a fractious Europe still lie within living memory. Rotterdam (*right*), where OMA is based, as it looked in 1940. The Nuremberg rally, 1936 (*opposite*); the Russians help take Berlin in 1945.

The 'European project' begins with the European Economic Community, established with the Treaty of Rome in 1957. With the fall of the Berlin Wall in 1989 (*right*) and the end of Communism, a united Europe becomes truly possible.

OMA

Are there twenty-eight national varieties of living
room, or is European domesticity the product of
an international network of design, manufacturing
and trade?

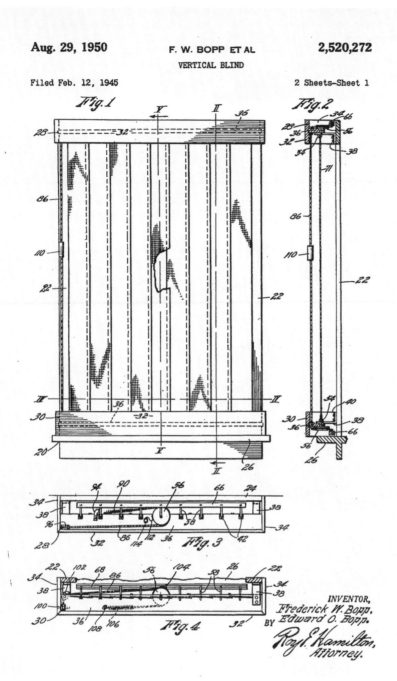

A patent drawing for the vertical blind, a ubiquitous screening device in which all the parts work in synchrony. When one slat is broken (*right*) the system becomes dysfunctional.

A room with furniture from the twenty-eight EU member states, and the vertical blind system, rendered as the barcode flag, concealing the bloody recent past of European history.

Empathy

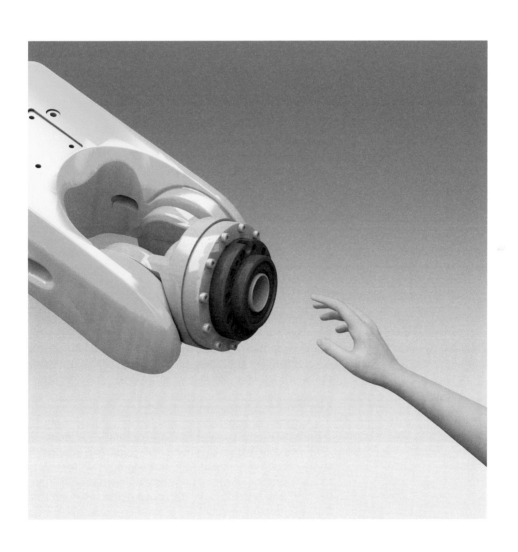

Meshing
JM Ledgard

'The new milieu [of advanced technology] has its own specific laws which are not the laws of organic or inorganic matter.' So wrote the French philosopher, Jacques Ellul. This was back in 1954, well before the trillionfold increase in computing power and its distribution down from government facility to factory, office, home, pocket and body were obvious to anyone. Ellul, who died in 1994, was concerned with human freedom in the face of technology. If he continues to speak to us with some force today it is precisely because his focus was on the interplay between the human and the machine. What assemblages are we? What happens to us in an automated world?

But first, what do we mean by automation? For a long time, it was a simple action – an automatic rifle. Then it became something smarter – a drip-feed irrigation system. Now we mean something closer to autonomy. Whereas in the past automation was a standard means to achieve a predetermined result, now automation is a non-standardized means to achieve outcomes that are always changing. Roboticists talk endlessly about autonomy. For them, there are layers and layers of autonomy. For our purposes, we can broadly define autonomous systems as those that perform tasks at a similar or superior level to humans. Autonomous systems already exist in the military and in space. The United States military has a pilotless helicopter called the K-Max, which has delivered thousands of tonnes of supplies under fire in the battlefields of Afghanistan and Iraq. Many forms of public transport are autonomous. Car manufacturers, such as Tesla and Mercedes, have introduced high-end vehicles that can drive autonomously. The driver is redundant. The car overtakes, even on motorways; it parks itself. Hundreds more autonomous systems will enter our lives in the next decade, whether we wish it or not. Most will be pushed by permission-less businesses built on leveraging the law for scale. These companies – Uber is one – identify an opportunity, raise vast sums on the logic of it, then use lawyers to scythe down government and civic opposition.

Autonomy accelerates, its terms defined only by available energy; it pushes towards more complexity, more connections, and gives the effect of slicing up space and time from top to bottom – so plunging us in scales from star system to quark, aeon to nanosecond. As Ellul suggested, there is a strange propulsion in play. It is hard to see, this propulsion, or even to understand if it is a law in the way that gravity is a law. Maybe it is the case that any task creates uncalled for tasks, or maybe it is something like that experienced in the financial world, which is propelled onwards by obscure counterparty obligations. It seemingly has

Empathy

The Redline Droneport project in Africa, designed by Foster + Partners, is intended to support cargo-drone routes capable of delivering urgent or essential supplies to remote areas on a massive scale.

its own agenda, which is not the agenda of living creatures known to us but is directed towards interstellar space, as if its only intention is to use us as hosts in the spreading of life (maybe just the vast biota of microbial life). If we are glum, we might say that we unconsciously set this process under way with the first cutting of an irrigation ditch in ancient Sumer – or even earlier, with the first sizzle of meat on a cave fire in the African Rift Valley.

I start at this point, at the deep end, because it is clear that everything is about to change. Steam set us up, electricity set us off, nuclear power and space set us apart, computing connected us; in parallel, we decoded the genome and now we move from being connected by technology to being meshed with technology, and the question is: who is meshing who?

Droneports

A few years ago, I left my job as a foreign correspondent to work on advanced technologies at the avant-garde École Polytechnique Fédérale de Lausanne (EPFL) in Switzerland. I wanted to see what was coming next, and have some small impact on futuristic thinking in emerging parts of the planet. That led me to robotics. I founded the Redline group to invent the droneport and build the world's first cargo drone route – in Africa. Several start-ups are now flying emergency supplies around in rural Africa, Airbus is getting involved, a droneport prototype has been constructed at the Venice Biennale and the first route will break ground in Rwanda. The crafts themselves will be cheap robots, autonomously flying precious cargo on fixed routes in the lower sky, droneport to droneport, town to town, across lakes, between mountains, down rivers to connect communities at motorbike prices. This is possible because the smartphone industry has commodified computing for smartphones – the brain of a Redline cargo drone will cost less than $100. In design, they will be rugged, cheap, fixed-wing, with six-metre wingspans, beautiful, quiet, silvery, streaming red LED lights behind them: the love child of Citroën 2CV and a *Star Wars* fighter who fell for each other in a seedy bar. Similarly, the droneport, as conceived by the design lead of Redline, Lord Norman Foster, will be a large, civic building of tiles compacted from soil dug on the site, costing no more to build than a petrol station, using sophisticated geometry and local labour, and including a digital-fabrication repair shop, pharmacy, postal service, and trading and e-commerce posts, sitting lightly on the earth, solar powered, with craft gliding in and out with emergency medicines, spare parts, e-commerce goods – meshing.

JM Ledgard

One of the purported aims of Google's self-driving car is to reduce traffic accidents—more than 1.2 million worldwide every year—as ninety-four per cent of accidents in the US involve human error.

Flying robotics has become a big industry very quickly. The Chinese drone manufacturer, DJI, unheard of five years ago, now has a $10 billion valuation. Given their cheap price and aerial capabilities, it is inevitable that drones will do a significant amount of the gathering and distribution of information and goods at a planetary level. It is reasonable to suggest that the 2020s could be for droneports in Africa what the 1840s were for railway stations in Europe. Though this is a relatively crude undertaking compared with what else is coming, and only serves to supplement roads and rail, there are still common signatures of the near future: better results at fractional cost, dematerialization of infrastructure, and renewed local production (according to Neil Gershenfeld of MIT's Centre for Bits and Atoms, a Redline droneport could, within a decade, routinely 'birth' the drones it needs in its own digital fab lab).

Themes of dematerialization and the mixing of small parts of advanced technology with large parts of low technology will proliferate. Everything is going to move faster, more cheaply, more accurately and transparently. What is physical wants to become virtual and what is virtual demands to manifest itself in the physical world. I cite here Autodesk, the company which developed the AutoCAD tool beloved of architects and engineers. The company is moving to the molecular level to develop nanorobots that can be injected into the body to attack cancers. 'Design in the inert world becomes design in the living world,' says Jeff Kowalski, the company's chief technology officer.

There is no room for techno-utopianism in our bare-fisted future, but Africa is coming online just as robotics is coming online. As fast as Africa develops, robotics will develop still faster. Robots will have negative implications for employment in industrial countries, but in non-industrial countries they can buy you an efficiency you could not otherwise afford. I started to think this way when I interviewed an al-Qaeda Shabab commander on a part of the malarial Jubba river on a trip to Somalia in 2009. It was during a famine. There was hunger everywhere. Girls sent to the river to fetch water were being eaten by large crocodiles. Waterborne diseases were wasting malnourished infants. The jihadists were beheading their enemies in surrounding villages. It was hard to imagine a society more broken down than that place at that time, yet the jihadist commander sat in his plastic chair with two mobile phones working off separate networks. That showed me that if a system is valuable enough, it will protect itself. It also suggested that new forms of technology had a resilience (persistence, insistence) that machinery had heretofore lacked in Africa.

Empathy

Eric was the UK's first robot—and one of the world's first robots. It was built by Captain WH Richards and AH Reffell, and publicly presented at the Model Engineering Exhibition in London in 1928.

Universal Robots

My time in the labs at EPFL and reading paper abstracts from robotics, computing, mathematics, physics and neuroscience journals put me in awe of the raw brain power of science, but it also unexpectedly reinforced my faith in imagination. A lot of science, it seems to me, tries to identify a narrative and run with it (e.g. dark matter), and the arrangement of experiments is at its base level just as much storytelling as Odysseus relating how he blinded the cyclops, Polyphemus. This is especially true of robotics. More than any other field of modern endeavour, the form and design of robots has been shaped in advance by culture. Several robotics professors I know confess that they got into the field because they wanted to bring R2D2 into the world. The word 'robot' first appeared in a stage play called *R.U.R.*, or *Rossum's Universal Robots*, by the Czech writer Karel Čapek. The play premiered in Prague in 1921, and made an immediate and lasting international impact; in 1938, it was the first piece of science fiction ever broadcast on BBC television. In the play, a scientific discovery on a tropical island allows for the molecular reassembly of life, and thus cheap robots. Hundreds of thousands of robots are shipped off to customers, satisfying the childlike desire, as in the Brothers Grimm's *The Elves and the Shoemaker*, that the work will be done while we sleep. R.U.R. slogans – 'Robots for the tropics!', 'Do you want to cheapen your output? Order Rossum's Robots' – speak to our well-founded angst that automation will do away with our careers (it will).

There is a lot in Čapek which reinforces the charge that technology too often takes complex means for careless ends. The robot butler serving the elite in the play brings to mind the CEO of Facebook, Mark Zuckerberg, who has taken as his hobby in 2016 the creation of an Artificial Intelligence (AI) that can serve as his butler. But the lasting contribution of *R.U.R.* is the framing of the entire technology of robots around work. 'Robot' comes from the Czech *robota*, meaning drudgery – drudge work of the kind that needs to be endlessly repeated in farms and homes (and of the home, I think of the coal smoke in Prague at that time; how Franz Kafka describes the windowsill of his apartment, always having a fresh layer of soot each morning; the prevalence of tuberculosis; widespread incapacity, again with the figure of the bedridden Kafka; and always, the need for changing shirt collars and washing clothes and sheets).

Robots do the vacuum cleaning in *R.U.R.*, and it is with some irony that I realized that the first mass application of robots on Earth has been – vacuuming. I recently sat on a panel in Boston

JM Ledgard

With the appearance of a baby harp seal and a plush coat of antibacterial fur, Paro is an interactive therapeutic robot designed to comfort elderly patients with cognition disorders.

The Roomba 980 is the first vacuum-cleaning robot to combine adaptive navigation with visual localization, and cloud-connected app control.

with Helen Greiner, co-founder of iRobot, the company that designed the first and most successful robot vacuum cleaner, Roomba, with more than fifteen million units sold. She told me that two-thirds of Roomba owners give their robot a name, and there is indeed a disorientation to hearing a vacuum cleaner in a room and seeing whoever you thought was running it appear out of another part of the house (this disconnection of human from task in the home deserves a new word).

Robot Laws
What rules should govern the design of robots? The popular starting point is the science fiction writer Isaac Asimov's Three Laws of Robotics:

1
A robot may not injure a human being or, through inaction, allow a human being to come to harm.

2
A robot must obey the orders given it by human beings except where such orders would conflict with the First Law.

3
A robot must protect its own existence as long as such protection does not conflict with the First or Second Laws.

Asimov's laws are not very useful for roboticists or lawyers. A robot cannot know all the ways in which any given order will affect a human. A robot cannot know all the orders given to it. A robot is fallible, and more so than a human given the problem of language and mutual understanding. The robotics track of UK Research has identified five principles of robotics for the near future:

1
Only the military gets to play war with robots. Robots should be used as weapons only for national security use. Governance of these weapons systems should be limited in similar ways to nuclear, biological, and

Empathy

The Valkyrie robot, created by NASA, is the first bipedal humanoid robot designed to support astronauts in space flights and future ground missions to Mars.

chemical weapons. [This is hard, given that warbots are miniature, affordable to non-state actors and impossible to track.]

2
Robots should obey the law through design. Robots are the agents of humans, who answer to the law. Robots are not legally culpable. [They are not even children but more like animals, for whom a 'feral moment' can mean being put down.]

3
Robots are products like cars and should be designed according to the highest levels of safety and security.

4
Robots should be designed 'so that their machine nature is transparent'. Robots should not through design take advantage of the vulnerable – for instance, confusing the elderly with messages of love. [How transparent should their machine nature be? There is no clear answer from roboticists, so far.]

5
Robots should be licensed. It should be easy to see who is legally responsible for any given robot. [Cargo drones should have illuminated markings.]

There are other issues. Technically, it seems that the movement of a robot and its intelligence have to be in synch or humans will be repulsed. Economically, it is still far too expensive to buy the dexterity required of a useful robot. New approaches are needed, and they will involve a lot of expensive coding. This will happen. While the legal implications of a homebot plunging a carving knife into its owner will be problematic, more difficult legal questions have already been solved – such as dividing up liability between jet engine, plane, airline, and pilot in an air crash.

On Valkyries
Domestic robots will be a $3 billion market by 2020. These will include cleaner robots, security robots, 3D printers, sex robots and family-friendly robots that offer interaction for children and

JM Ledgard

The private company Space X, founded by Elon Musk, plans to launch its first mission to Mars with the Dragon spacecraft in 2018. It hopes to send humans by 2024.

The New York-based Team Space Exploration Architecture, and Clouds Architecture Office of New York, won NASA's 3-D Printed Habitat Challenge design competition in 2015 with their Mars Ice House.

the elderly. Two family bots – Buddy and Jibo – are already on the market. Robots for dementia patients will be a lucrative business. Some, such as Paro a cuddly seal-pup robot, will offer therapy in animatronic form. Sales of industry, medical and military robots will exceed those of domestic bots by tenfold or more, but the more significant robots for us as a species will be space robots. Here, NASA's Valkyrie programme is instructive. Valkyrie is a humanoid robot designed to prepare for habitation on Mars in advance of human arrival. Valkyries will also maintain the shelters once humans are on the Red Planet. The first Valkyrie is fully electric, 1.8 metres high, 90 kilos, with numerous torque-controlled joints offering a high degree of freedom of movement, and with many cameras and sensors (six on each palm, and eight along each of its four fingers). Several universities, including Edinburgh and MIT, have received their own Valkyrie to play with. 'If we can integrate the autonomy work with our planning and control algorithms, it could result in an unprecedented level of autonomous capabilities for a humanoid robot,' says Russ Tendrake, head of the robot locomotion group at MIT's Computer Science and Artificial Intelligence Laboratory (CSAIL). In other words, a cool robot at last.

Valkyries are crazily named after the Norse women supernaturals who decided who would be slain in battle and who would survive. They then took the dead with them to Odin's Valhalla and Freyja's Folkvangr. What is going on here? Are Valkyrie robots gendered? Is there something they are trying to tell us? That the escape out of this solar system is the battle, and robots will decide who lives and dies? We can assume that by 2034, Valkyries and similar proxies will be able to access the available AI of the planet and work through the data seamlessly and ceaselessly as required. Valkyries' first work could be with ice on Mars: extruding a shelter thick enough to act as a radiation shield but thin enough in parts to be translucent for the humans living within it. That is the idea of NASA's Mars Ice House. The concept takes account of Martian physics to 3D print ice into tall, conical shelters. Most of the technology required for this already exists. The rest will be perfected by private space explorers led by Elon Musk's Space X. Musk, who also owns the Tesla electric car company, is beginning an unprecedented acceleration of privately funded space travel using recycled rockets. The aim is to take advantage of the narrowing of the Earth–Mars orbit in the 2030s. The leap to Mars will take place around the year 2034. It will require daily rocket launches of supplies in the preceding years, many of the launches from newly established spaceports

Empathy

Kaman has been developing the Unmanned K-MAX since 1998. It was developed for hazardous missions, including delivering supplies to the battlefield in situations involving chemical, biological or radiological risks.

in equatorial Africa. Here then, with Valkyries and the Red Planet, is another truth we can lock in about the near future: what we once talked about we will now accomplish, and Mars will become a political and economic reality to Earth, just as Virginia became true to Elizabethan England.

There will be No Deckard

The reliance on artificial intelligence and robots for our push outwards towards the Kuiper Belt underlines the painful truth that our fleeting forms and instantly decaying brains are not fit for purpose. Some of these questions are raised in *Blade Runner*, Ridley Scott's 1982 film based on a story by the writer Philip K Dick. The main characters are a bounty hunter, Deckard, and a 'replicant' (a bioengineered android), Roy Batty. Deckard hunts down Batty. Leaving aside the implausible economics of having something as well made as Batty switch off, the culminating tears-in-the-rain monologue, in which Batty dies, is unfading. As human Deckard clings to a building by his fingertips, replicant Batty stares down at him curiously and finally speaks: 'Quite an experience to live in fear, isn't it? That's what it is to be a slave.'

The point of this, from today's perspective, is quite different from what was intended in 1982. No one then challenged the ascendancy of the human. It was about asking questions of replicant self-awareness. Batty's inception date is given as 8 January 2016. If that is optimistic, so is the rest of the film. The question for us is not whether the replicant will exist, but rather will the human recognizably survive in the near future. Our desire for immortality; our wish to soup up our intelligence and endurance; and our readiness to absorb bionic parts, animal parts and hyperphysical realities make it all but certain that there will be no Deckard and no Batty, but something meshed together. We have gone just about as far as a wet brain can go. We are not fit for interstellar travel. To get out there we – or it – will have to dematerialize ourselves – or itself; our minds will have to go to the cloud. This is already happening. Google's Deep Mind AI division are beginning to investigate how episodic memories can be uploaded into the cloud and shared across a network. This is fearful for us. We fear being apart from each other, but we also fear losing control.

The Future will be Human

We can talk about the way Valkyries are coming for us, or our species leap, but the immediate future will be messily human. In industrialized countries, there are not going to be enough

JM Ledgard

Flight Assembled Architecture is a research project by Gramazio Kohler Architects and Raffaello D'Andrea, exploring the future of building construction by flying robots. The project was exhibited in 2012 at the FRAC Centre in Orleans, France.

jobs. Fifty per cent of jobs may be susceptible to automation. As Thomas Piketty and others have shown, the last doubling of productivity has enriched only a few. It is no coincidence that substance abuse and suicide has driven up mortality rates of white US men since 1990 – nor is it a surprise that many of those same men reach out to the unworkable, nativist politics championed by Republican presidential nominee Donald Trump.

At a planetary level, we can lock in human population growth at the highest end of UN predictions. That makes everything more combustible. Africa's fertility rate is twice the planetary average. There were 490 million Africans in 1984 – the year of the Ethiopian famine and Band Aid. There will be 1.8 billion Africans in 2034 – the first year of the anticipated Martian colony. Most of these new Africans will live in towns that are yet to be built. Most will not find a salaried job. Their migration to Europe will be restricted with lethal force. Climate change and ruined soils will lead to periodic spikes in food prices. There are as yet unknown effects of the loss of grasses and pollinating insects, and other life forms in the face of the spreading Anthropocene. African economies are slipping back. Terms of trade are mostly negative. $18 billion of sovereign bonds will be hard to refinance. Poverty and disease burden remain extreme. In this context, a rise in political, Pentecostalist and Islamist groups is likely, and atrocities carried out by such groups can be expected.

So you have these divergent trends: Valkyries building ice houses on Mars, while a great density of human life blooms in the tropics on Earth. The poor will not stand still. They will have access to knowledge and tools, just as the Valkyries will. Long before 2034, they will have stickers on the mastoid bone for universal language translation, smears on their neck and belly as anti-malarials and to increase mental and sexual performance, and implants into the skull for meshing – however that looks. There will be no more handsets; you will be your own identifier. Within a decade, we might see the end of coins, and in their place jewellery or tattoos loaded with digital value denominated to infinitesimal parts so that they can be pushed back and forward to pay for a visit to a latrine or a virtual reality English Premier League match (choose your player). However, the paradox identified with the droneport will still remain. A person will have access to a robot, but will not have clean water, or shelter, or safety. Whatever is technically scaleable will be scaled and what is not scaleable will have to be fought for, household by household.

Empathy

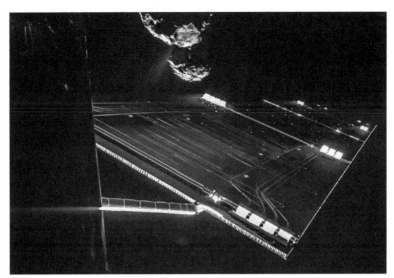

Rosetta

If we think that all this is far-fetched, we should remember the feat of the Rosetta spacecraft, which in 2015 deployed the Philae probe on to the surface of the comet 67P/Churyumov-Gerasimenko. Even more powerful, the Voyager I and II spacecrafts launched in 1977. Voyager I is now nineteen billion kilometres away from Earth. It is the first man-made object to enter interstellar space. Even travelling at the speed of light, it takes a day for its transmissions to reach us. It is alone: the next star system is 40,000 years away. It will outlast any part of our existing civilization: cricket, warm beer, Arthur Dent—all of it. Yet not quite. Because Voyager will surely be overtaken by faster spacecraft sent from Earth, and if it is not captured along the way and is allowed to continue at a snail's pace, its arrival at the star system will be a spectacle for whatever intelligence lives there then.

If indeed everything, at its base, is binary ones and zeros, and we have evolved to create and appreciate such beauty, there is no reason that there should not be a Keatsian AI. Similarly, banality will continue on also. A friend, the artist Olafur Eliasson, tried something interesting with the Chinese artist Ai Wewei. Together they created a virtual moon, and allowed anyone to leave a message on it online. The idea was to make a mark on a virtual world, a world you could imagine from any country. You can still find the moon online. What happened was that it became a kind of alleyway in which, like in classical Rome, people scrawled their marks; just names; or, more often, cocks and balls, ejaculations—the graffiti of humans in space.

Which brings us to love. What about love in an age of autonomy? It is surely going to be a much more useful emotion than fear. Fear can mandate and hold back some technologies, such as ethically extreme elements of the CRISPR gene-editing revolution, but it cannot direct us in the most important questions, which curiously remain most beautifully static in all this turbulence: why do we love, who do we love, how do we love?

Madeline Gannon
Mimus: Face to Face with our Companion Species

Madeline Gannon heads ATONATON, a research studio inventing better ways to communicate with machines. In her research, Gannon designs and implements cutting-edge tools that explore the future of digital making. Her work blends disciplinary knowledge from design, robotics and human-computer interaction to innovate at the edges of digital creativity. Gannon is completing a PhD in Computational Design at Carnegie Mellon University, where she is developing techniques for digitally designing and fabricating wearables on and around the body.

Tactum, self-designed and 3D-printed wearables, 2015

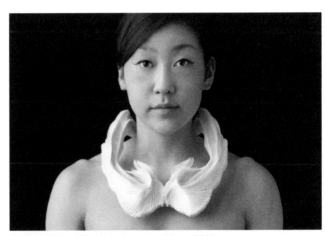

Reverb, 'Collar 03' soft elastomer prototype, 2014

Reverb, 'Collar 01' rigid nylon prototype, 2014

3D-scanning, modelling and printing software created by Madeline Gannon for Tactum and Reverb

Madeline Gannon

Automation represents the pinnacle of our technological progress, but it comes at the expense of our relevance to this world.

Automation drives down the cost of production, making products and services more available to more economically diverse groups of people. We may often think of automation in terms of producing luxury consumer goods, like cars, clothes, appliances and electronics. But it also impacts on the production of the most basic necessities of life, like food, medicine, and shelter. In the United States, automation in agriculture has reduced the number of jobs from forty per cent of the population in 1900 to less than one per cent today, with a twenty-five per cent surplus in production. Automation in medicine has contributed towards the discovery of new treatments,[1] new drugs,[2] and safer production processes.[3] And the automated production of construction materials such as plywood, insulation, gypsum board and concrete block has contributed to more structurally reliable buildings at lower costs.

The problem with automation is that the more effective it is, the more obsolete we become.

Machines built for automation do things for us: things we can't physically do, things too dangerous for us to do, things we don't want to do. They can work non-stop, they never get tired, they never complain, and they can't unionise … yet. In a global economy fuelled by the cost of labour, they are the perfect worker. Consequently, our technological progress comes at a great human cost: when automation moves into an industry, jobs are not displaced, they are eliminated. This disruption was first felt in the low-skill labour market, it is arriving in high-skill, blue-collar jobs, and is now reaching towards high-skill, white-collar jobs.[4] So why are we creating the means for our own obsolescence? If machines that do things *for* us also replace us—why not adapt these machines to do things *with* us?[5]

We have brought an industrial robot—the pre-eminent symbol of industrial automation—to live in the Design Museum for the duration of the exhibition. Traditionally, industrial robots are designed to do short, predetermined tasks at very high speeds, over and over again. For our installation, we have pushed the robot beyond its intended use and given it the ability to move autonomously throughout its environment. It has no predetermined tasks to do. Instead, its physical behaviours are generated in real time to acknowledge the crowd of visitors moving around it.

We approached the design of the installation as if we were bringing a wild animal into the gallery. And as is the case for zoos and menageries, the design of the installation is twofold: the staging and enclosure for the creature, and its interactions with visitors. For the physical design of the installation, the challenge was to integrate the necessary safety and sensing infrastructure in a way that still facilitated awe, wonder and spectacle when visitors interact with the machine.

When experiencing the installation, our greatest ambition is for visitors to momentarily forget that this is a machine and see it more as a living creature. To cultivate empathy between visitors and the robot, we have designed its movements to mimic how a captive animal might behave in a similar scenario. Using the robot's body language and posturing, we can communicate a spectrum of responses to a visitor: the robot may seem curious or shy; excited or indifferent; playful or agitated.

For most visitors, this installation will be the first time that they have ever seen an industrial robot in real life. For these people, our installation will offer the opportunity to make first contact between two species[6]—one human, one machinic—and to foster an awareness of each other's affordances and limitations. However, some visitors to the installation will likely feel the impact of similar machines on their livelihoods.[7] For these people, we hope to offer some form of reconciliation: with small, but strategic adaptations to our current automation systems, we can make these machines more than just a replacement for a person. Creating human-centred interfaces that cultivate one's personal connection to this machine, we aimed to show that a robot has the potential to be a companion, an apprentice, a collaborator or a partner in what we do. There are better, more inclusive methods for humans and robots to coexist with one another—we just need to realize them.

Design can challenge assumptions about the way things *are* and show ways in which they *could be*. As designers, we have the liberty to wander among different 'silos' of disciplinary knowledge and offer novel perspectives on entrenched problems. Our insatiable curiosity drives us to conceive and create worlds that are full of alternative futures.

1 Sam Michael *et al.*, 'A Robotic Platform for Quantitative High-Throughput Screening', *Assay and Drug Development Technologies* 6.5 (2008), 637–57.

2 Armaghan W. Naik *et al.*, 'Active machine learning-driven experimentation to determine compound effects on protein patterns', *eLife* 5 (2016).

3 Kevin Williams *et al.*, 'Cheaper faster drug development validated by the repositioning of drugs against neglected tropical diseases', *Journal of the Royal Society Interface* (2015).

4 Pew Research Center, *AI, Robotics, and the Future of Jobs* (2014).

5 Brookings Institute, *How Humans Respond to Robots: Building Public Policy through Good Design* (2014).

6 Illah R. Nourbakhsh, *Robot Futures*, (Cambridge, MA, 2013).

7 Pew Research Center, *Public Predictions for the Future of Workforce Automation* (2016).

Madeline Gannon

Industrial robots are inherently dangerous machines to work with: they operate at very high speeds with very high precision, and they have little-to-no awareness of the environment outside of their programmed tasks. Industrial robots thrive in highly controlled environments where they can be strictly separated from unpredictable objects, like people.

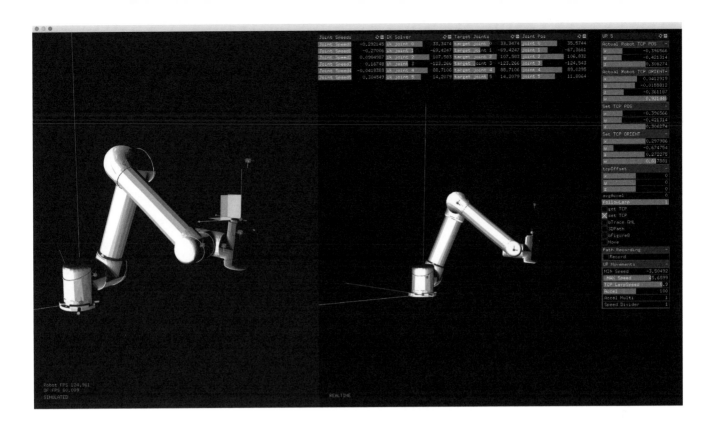

Madeline Gannon proposes two layers of software working together to create a spatial experience in her 'Mimus' installation. The first layer controls the robot, generating its movements 'on the fly' and in response to how visitors are moving around the installation. The second layer detects and tracks visitors to the installation with ceiling-mounted sensors.

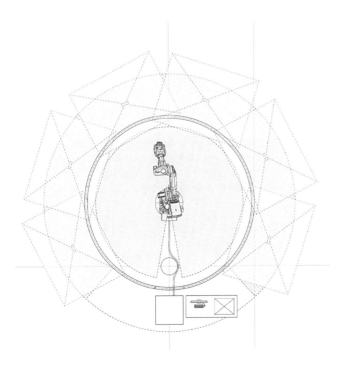

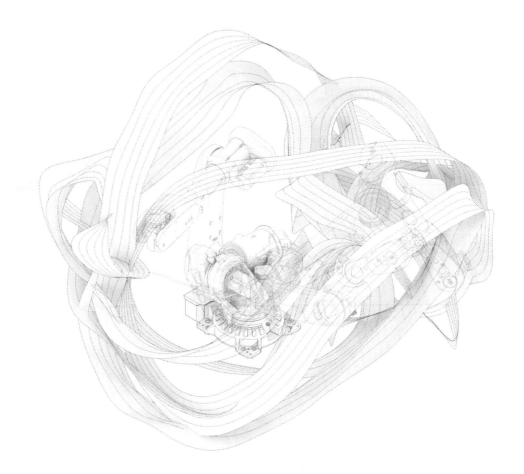

An industrial robot's movements are constrained
to a spheroid of space within its reach. Kinematically,
the robot moves in a manner that is not dissimilar
to that of a human arm. ABB's IRB 6700 robot has six
joints, or six degrees of freedom, that move in unison
to reach a point in space.

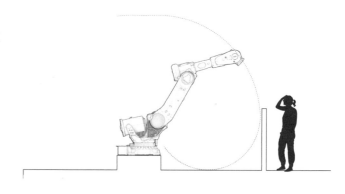

Once the robot receives a natural gesture from the
crowd of visitors, it moves to respond and engage with
them. The robot adapts its position, orientation, speed
and acceleration, creating a palette of postures.

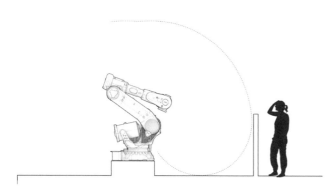

Empathy

Madeline Gannon in conversation with Gonzalo Herrero

GH   MG

Originally trained as an architect but currently working between product design and robot programming, you're not limited to a particular design discipline. Is it fair to say that?

> I've been building a career by wandering between these silos of disciplinary knowledge, whether it's architecture, robotics, computer science or design. The success I have had is being able to navigate the in-between spaces and trying to build a bridge between many different ways of thinking.

Your recent work navigates different formats and techniques, from 3D printing to robots and open software. What do they all share?

> Improving communication between humans and machines is a common thread that ties a lot of my work together. The motivation behind it is just to have more humanized interfaces for exploring things with these machines. Until very recently, the people who develop the ways that you might use a 3D printer, a CNC router or an industrial robot were engineers who might not be doing the sort of things that artists, architects or designers might want to be doing with them. When I first started working with these machines, I quickly hit a limitation in what I could explore because I was constrained by the software interface. So most of the motivation lies in finding ways to use these machines as an extension of my own creative explorations, as an extension of my own curiosities, and to integrate them into the way I think about problem solving, or the way I think about designing things.

What challenges do you tackle in your robotics work?

> Part of the problem of working with these machines is that a person has to think like a robot in order to use it. You have to make some abstraction between what you want to do, translate that into something that the robot can understand

GH   MG

> and then execute it. So the interfaces that I create invert that. We give the robot an understanding of the human's intention instead of vice versa. What I work towards is finding ways to build that closer connection between an industrial robot and a person.

And what are the possibilities of that approach?

> These industrial robots are really incredible machines. When they're used in factories they can be used at high speed and with high precision. They run non-stop, they don't complain, they never get hungry. What I'm working towards is, instead of thinking of this as a piece of machinery, to think of it as an apprentice for people doing more agile or more spontaneous work. These machines are so adaptable that you can put a different tool on the end of them and they can all of a sudden do a completely different thing, from lifting something to spraying something, from catching something to pushing something. It's like having another arm or like having another person to help you along. Additionally, I think one of the biggest potentials is for robotics to begin to revive dying or dead crafts. That's what a lot of people in architectural robotics are now exploring.

Is there a counterpart to all this?

> The problem now is that in the field of robotics proper, there are not many people asking these machines to do more than what they already can. They're mainly interested in finding better or more efficient or safer ways to do what they can already do. So it's more a question of optimization than appropriation. That, in some ways, is one of the benefits of coming from an outside domain. I can take the same knowledge set, the same toolset, and ask completely different questions of this technology that I find really interesting, and that people in other domains might find really interesting.

What effect will automation have
on the working environment?

If you think about robots just as these
arms that were around since the early
1970s, then we're quickly seeing a
progression of them automating a lot of
what used to be hand labour. But robotic
automation is something that happens
everywhere in a more abstract way than
in a factory setting. A great example for
understanding that automation is a
double-edged sword is the use of
drywall in the building industry. Prior to
drywall, you had a lot of plasterwork,
which is a beautiful medium—there's
a lot of embodied knowledge and you
need a lot of skill, you apprentice for
many years in order to perfectly render
a wall. And then you shift to this drywall
model where you have this huge assembly line where, with a lever, a single
person can cast a standardized panel.
The room around you is all drywall, you
don't even see the plasterwork in it, so
you see the death of one industry
and the rebirth of a new material that,
while it took away lots of jobs, is also
much cheaper to use. It drives down
housing costs, it adds fire resistance,
all these extra things that you get from
this engineered material. I think that
a lot of the fear that you get with robots,
and where I see the love for them, is
in this potential for unforeseen benefits.
There's a cost to it, but there can also
be a reward.

How does your project respond
to *Fear and Love*?

When we go to see a lion at the zoo,
we're excited to see it, but then when it
starts coming up to the glass we get a
little bit more concerned and we step
back—we trust that the enclosure works
because someone designed it, but we
oscillate between anxiety and fascina-
tion with this creature that we don't quite
understand. We feel that if we sit there
and stare at it for long enough we can
build some kind of awareness of what
it is, what it wants and how it moves.
The interaction that we've developed for
this project is quite similar. We're relying
on communicating a lot, and building
this more emotive connection between
the visitor and the robot through body
language. The way that we're

approaching this is to have it be driven
by sensors in the environment. So the
robot is seeing you and the whole crowd
simultaneously, then it begins to pick
and choose who to engage with and how
to engage in that scenario through
the sensing and computer vision that
we have installed in the environment.

What sort of emotions will this project
provoke in the visitor?

Personally, I have the whole spectrum of
emotions for these machines. That's why
I don't say that we're training the robot
to do something, I say that we're taming
it. We're taming this technology because
it does have a wild side to it. We're still
asking it to do something that this
machine was never designed to do.
So I think that we should have a healthy
anxiety about these machines, for
instance in eliminating human labour or
taking us out of the equation. The very
basic objective is just building awareness of what this thing is and what it can
do, and also hopefully alleviating some
anxiety and showing that it's just a
machine. It just does what we tell it to
do—there's no sentience to it.

What are the questions raised in
this project?

For me, what's exciting is to expand
the debate outside the museum.
What comes of this project is the emotional connection that a person can
have with this machine, which is entirely
one-sided as this machine can feel no
emotion towards a person. But, because
we can control its posturing and communicate things with its body language,
that response will just happen. Whether
it is adoration or fear is really exciting.
This project is expected to provoke many
questions around it. First, what is an
industrial robot doing into a gallery? But
also, what's the design aspect of it?
Is the viewer's emotional response being
manipulated by the designer? I'm eager
to leave space for interpretation.

With 'Quipt', Madeline Gannon created a human-centred interface for collaborating with industrial robots: instead of programming a robot through code, 'Quipt' lets you communicate with an industrial robot using your body language. Motion-capture cameras track markers worn on your hands, neck or body, and then feed their world positions to the robot so that it can see and respond to you in a shared space.

Madeline Gannon

Metahaven
A Love Letter to Sea Shepherd

Metahaven was founded in 2007 by Vinca Kruk and Daniel van der Velden. They first collaborated on a speculative visual design for the Principality of Sealand, an unrecognized mini-state on a former military structure in the North Sea that tried to reinvent itself as an internet-hosting platform. This led to the publication of *Uncorporate Identity* (2010), a book that, according to the *New York Times*, 'questions the purpose and value of design in a neurotic and treacherous era of geopolitical instability'. Its successor, *Can Jokes Bring Down Governments?* (2013), examines internet memes as a contemporary tactic of political protest. In 2011, Metahaven created a collection of scarves and T-shirts in support of WikiLeaks that has been widely published.

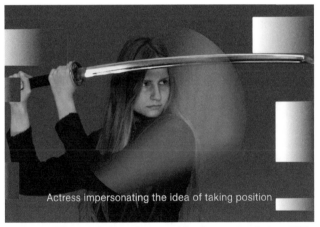

The Sprawl (Propaganda About Propaganda), a documentary feature, 2016

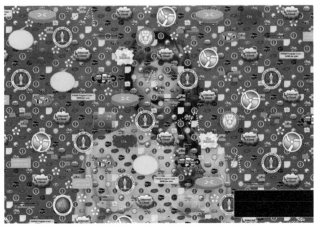

Video for 'Home', from Holly Herndon's 2015 album *Platform*

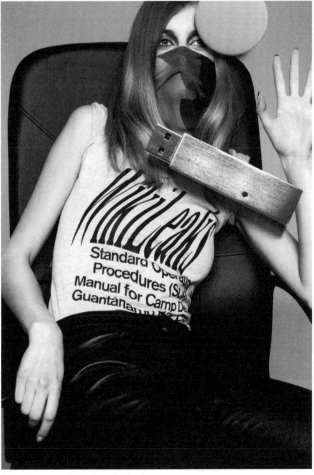

Branding campaign for Wikileaks, 2011

Metahaven

In March, 2016, the *New York Times* wrote in its review of the Oculus Rift virtual-reality (VR) headset: '…But a reality in which you are a dead pilot enslaved to fight and die over and over? Hard-core gamers may love this, but I prefer to be in a less depressing place when escaping from actual reality. Put me on a beach where I can look at whales.'[1]

Whales, hugely intelligent mammals that are hunted down and killed by humans, are, today, currency in a virtual-reality economy of immersion and affect. Whales do not need to be alive to fulfil their role in our imaginary. As pixel-creatures in 4K definition, they are most convincing; just put on your VR glasses and feel the love, while the actual oceans are being depleted of life. A humpback whale is an insurance commercial[2] – fuzzy, Zen spirituality for the disenfranchised. The aesthetic fetish of the whale silently takes part in the larger process of its extinction.

In a sense, the whale represents a key problem of modern design. Our increasing abilities to visualize, aestheticize and design, to shape pixels and virtual realities on screens and surfaces, are inversely proportional to our abilities to have a positive impact on the state of the world as it evolves; the space in which we feel something is disconnected from the space in which we do something.

Sea Shepherd know this. They are a direct action group founded by Paul Watson. The organization intervenes directly and physically to prevent and obstruct illegal whale-hunting in the Pacific and Antarctic regions. Sea Shepherd is different from environmental NGOs such as Greenpeace (which was also co-founded by Watson, before Sea Shepherd existed). While Greenpeace sometimes appears as a mainstream consumer brand, mirroring the corporate policies that it criticizes, Sea Shepherd occupies a pirate-like outsider position. Its logo is a skull adorned with tridents. Its ships, used to ram whaling vessels, are painted in grey dazzle and camouflage. At the foundation of Sea Shepherd lies an encounter with a whale:

In the early seventies, [Paul] *Watson, along with some two dozen other environmental activists, created Greenpeace. In 1975, alarmed by the declining number of whales, the group decided to confront a Soviet whaling fleet off the coast of California. Their plan was to use Zodiacs to put themselves between the harpooners and the whales. When Greenpeace caught up with the fleet, Watson jumped into a Zodiac with Fred Easton, a cameraman. The two men witnessed a Soviet harpooner firing into a pod of whales. At one point, an injured sperm whale charged toward them. 'It scared the hell out of us in the beginning,' Easton said. 'I just remember Paul saying, "Here he comes!," and we sat there. I couldn't get my camera going, and we both sat at the edge of the Zodiac, on the other side of which the whale was approaching. He swam right past us, and I swear to God he couldn't have been any more than ten feet away, and he was a huge male sperm whale, and he had an eye about the size of a dinner plate, and he did look at us with some sort of compassion, in the sense that he was certainly capable of doing harm to us in the circumstances, and had he been human we*

might have expected him to.' The two men, watching the whale swim away, were overcome with emotion. 'In an instant, my life was transformed and a purpose for my life was reverently established,' Watson later wrote.[3]

Watson's suggestion that the animal had empathy with the human reverses conventional wisdom, in which we are always the ones to care. With Sea Shepherd, we confront the devastating results of our own intervention into nature – the impact of our own design – and the mysterious force of the non-human counterpart that is the whale – sublime and epic, irreducible to beauty (or pixels), unintelligible to the human syntax. Sea Shepherd, seen through a design lens, is not just about the fight to save the whales (a fight which must be won), but about our relationship with all non-human consciousness – be it animals, or artificial intelligence.

Indeed, the boyish-looking Korean Go champion Lee Sedol was in tears when, in March 2016, he beat a most formidable opponent – the self-learning, never-resting Google DeepMind AlphaGo, 'a piece of distributed software supported by a team of more than 100 scientists.'[4] Lee beat the AI algorithm once in a series of five matches, the other four of which he lost.

There is an under-explored connection between the different ways in which we treat non-human forms of intelligence. On the one hand we are empathizing with machines, and teaching them how to exhibit behavior that we find desirable. We seem obsessed with comparing our own intelligence to that of computers, and with organizing a competition between the two. On the other hand, there are forms of intelligence that we barely understand and continue to destroy.

Our project for Sea Shepherd reflects a desire to extend this vision – the connection between animal and artificial intelligence – into design objects and strategies.

Like every organization, Sea Shepherd makes its presence known through actions in the world. We wish to expand on its current repertoire of forms to create a militantly fashionable visual brand that acknowledges and admits to the inabilities of contemporary design to affect the world's ecological realities, visually deconstructs and recreates the encounter with the 'whale AI', and creates a new space in which to realize the vast unknown space of life forms – natural and artificial – that are not understood by humans. In this project we, most of all, create a space in which to feel new things; the way in which these things then connect to what we can and must concretely *do* is through helping Sea Shepherd do what it does.

1 Brian X Chen, 'Oculus Rift Review: A Clunky Portal to a Promising Virtual Reality', *New York Times* (March 28, 2016).

2 Pacific Life, trailer for 3D documentary *Humpback Whales* (February 11, 2015).

3 Raffi Khatchadourian, 'Neptune's Navy: Paul Watson's wild crusade to save the oceans', *New Yorker* (November 5, 2007).

4 Christopher Moyer, 'How Google's AlphaGo Beat a Go World Champion: Inside a man-versus machine showdown', *Atlantic* (March 28, 2016).

The annual *grindadráp* whale hunting ceremony in
the Faroe Islands, which has been disrupted by Sea
Shepherd a number of times. This image, shot by
Adam Woolfitt in 1970, caused controversy when it
was published in *National Geographic* magazine.

Japanese whaling vessels often brand their ships with the word 'research' to avoid being challenged. The Sea Shepherd trimaran Ady Gil (*below*) was rammed and sunk by one such vessel, Shonan Maru 2, in 2010.

Paul Watson (*below*), the founder of the Sea Shepherd Conservation Society, photographed in 1983

Empathy

The logo was designed by Geert Vons, artistic
director of Sea Shepherd. It plays on the long history
of skull-and-crossbones insignias, replacing the bones
with a trident and a shepherd's crook.

Mugs, the default standard of merchandising.
And yet the branding manages to avoid looking like
the product of a marketing department.

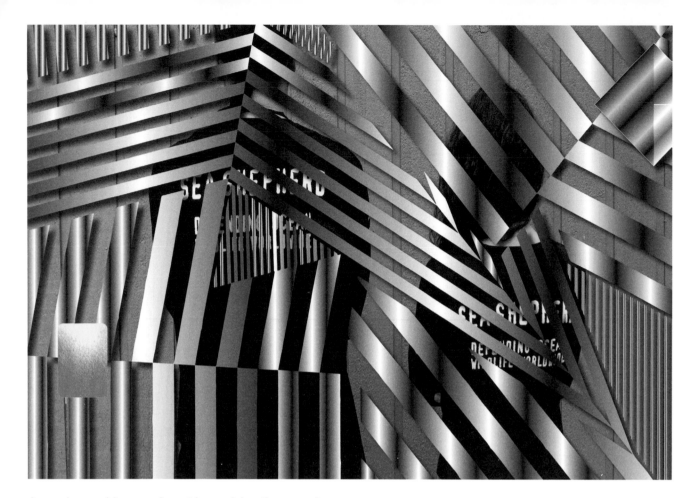

An early graphic experiment in applying the group's
use of dazzle painting on its vessels

Metahaven in conversation with Gonzalo Herrero

GH   M

GH   M

You are known for your politically engaged work, and most recently for your film making. Do you think you reflect a shift in graphic design today?

It's very hard to define graphic design today. A lot of politically engaged graphic design today is actually produced without the name 'graphic design' attached to it. We think that's actually the graphic design that we are particularly interested in. Within some circles, there's nostalgia for a time when politically engaged design announced itself – you had a poster that called for a strike, it did stuff. Now, maybe videos and social media perform these roles, but in a much more complex way. For us, film making is an extension of graphic design. We already work with lectures – telling stories, making images for them – and these became like mini-documentaries. You could say that graphic design, or design, is ultimately a means to solve a problem, to tell a story, to highlight a problem or provoke a response. Ultimately, the shift that is happening is maybe that there is less reliance on problems as they are formulated for designers by experts, and there is more emphasis on designers actually playing a role in formulating those problems themselves, and then also hopefully doing something about them. So that's a major shift.

Is humour in your projects a strategy to create empathy when talking about politics? Is it a way of softening the message in some way, making it more accessible?

We think humour is a way of compensating for the lack of power that we have as designers. We may not have a direct political influence but we do have the power of other things; imagination, imagery, strategy and humour are a very important part of that. So, I would say it's not necessarily a way to soften, but maybe it's a way to sharpen, or compensate for the lack of direct political influence that we wish we could have.

It's a way to hijack or reappropriate or infiltrate.
But we also see that those tactics have been adopted by governments and by the secret service, and by terrorist groups. They have mastered the art of the meme, the art of the troll – all these things that started with Anonymous, with a citizen-centred resistance. So we are currently living through a very deep cynicism with the internet, where we know that in all its layers it is penetrated with propaganda and with people who are strategizing to achieve certain goals. From twitter-bots to fake videos to entire campaigns, and it's everywhere. Recently, we made a visit to Mexico and presented some stuff from this film we did, *The Sprawl*, which has lots of examples of these bots from Russia, and people said, 'You should make this about Mexico,' because Mexico has sixty to seventy thousand twitter-bots for the president, which flood the internet with hashtags that destroy the possibilities of protest because the hashtag has been polluted with meaningless pictures of flowers. So this is Anonymous in service of the status quo.

So do you think design can create political or social change?

Definitely, because 'design' also means that. It also means a plan or plot; it's not just a layout, taste or aesthetics. So anything that involves a plan is a form of design. Especially for designers who are part of a group of people or movement that actually wants to make these changes. That's not the same as saying: I'm a great designer so we deal with these types of visual problems. No, it's saying: I'm a designer and I'm personally, politically part of a group in society that wants to see these things happening.

In your work on WikiLeaks, you contacted the designer, Aska, whom Julian Assange commissioned to design its visual identity. The brief was to design a logo that would connect with people on an emotional level. The power of design to engage the emotions is a subtext of this show – hence, *Fear and Love*. Does looking at design through fear and love resonate with you, or seem like a valid reflection of our time?

We think they are very important terms for design, in this world where you constantly have to produce and there is so much competition as well. We don't think anything else could keep you going. And the commitment that you could call love, not only the love that we share with our partners but also through our work and our commitment to topics, commitment to causes, commitment to making something. Fear is also, from a completely different angle, really important. We wouldn't say a driving force, but maybe it's a provoking force, this constant exploration of fear, and fear of something that needs a new solution or that poses new questions and creates new situations. It feels like they are very broad terms. What we like about them is that they sound like a music album, the album that New Order never made.

We think that there's been a heavy investment in terms of emotion by market-driven forces in visual culture. Where you say that everything has to look magenta in order to engage with our passions, or whatever … bullshit, of course. This is an important opportunity for design to take back those terms and see how they can be iterated differently than creating 'magenta identities'. There's a lot of pre-emption going on in our culture – in design, politics, etc. Possibilities have to be acted upon before they become actual.

How is that position represented in the project you made for this exhibition?

For a long time, we have wanted to work for Sea Shepherd, just because what they do is absolutely necessary. They are a group that intervenes directly in the act of killing whales, and is not interested in playing the card of the politically

correct NGO or the group that can talk to everyone. Their speech is action, it's direct. And for them, the human is not the most important figure in nature – they move away from a human-oriented focus. So that's why we chose, on the one hand, to make stuff for Sea Shepherd that they can use, and on the other hand to connect Sea Shepherd to the idea of non-human consciousness, which also speaks to emotion. Our main example there is currently the Go match between Lee Sedol and Google DeepMind – a human against a computer. One time, the computer wins, and the other time the human wins, and so on.

How would you describe this project in a single sentence?

We need to iterate it a few times… We think that whales themselves are the prime examples of this affect-driven commercial visual culture. Not as in the actual living, breathing species, but as in visual objects that you can use to trigger certain emotions – whether it's through their song or their appearance, their intelligence, their majesty. All these things are used to create virtual worlds, in a way, to create something super nice in 3D and 4D environments. Whereas the real story is a sea full of plastic and a few leftover species that can survive in that. The first whales have been found that have ingested lots of plastic; it's horrible. So whales exist exactly on this knife-edge between fear and love.

The dazzle-painted Bob Barker, named after the
American television game show host and animal rights
activist, in the Antarctic as part of Operation Zero
Tolerance in 2013.

Empathy, which is essential to identifying with non-human intelligence (whether whales or artificial intelligence), is turned into a graphic identity using Sea Shepherd patches and dazzle camouflage.

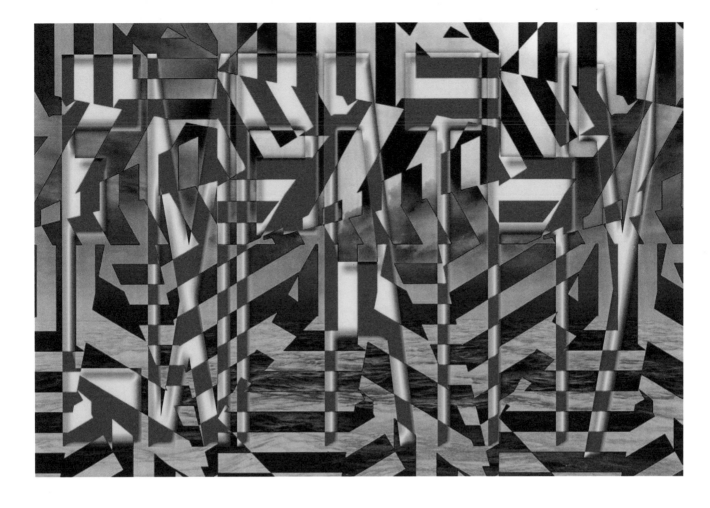

Steps towards an online campaign that uses
'captcha' tests to prove that you are human,
and thus have empathy

Early sketches (*opposite*) on the theme of fear
and love. These play with the idea of the whale as
an 'iconic' image, and our obsession with creating
high-definition simulations of the environment
as we continue to destroy it.

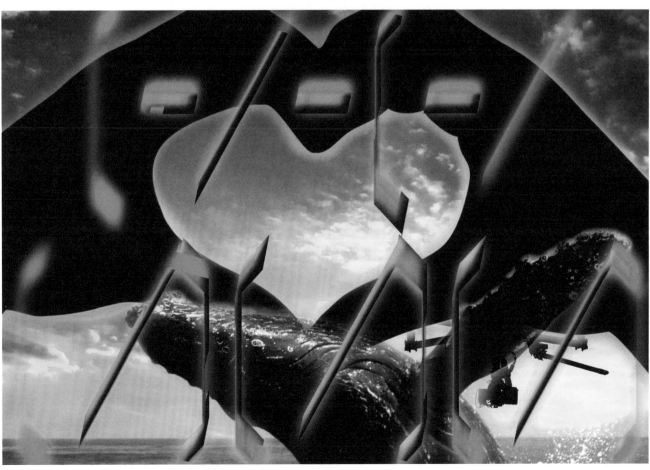

Body

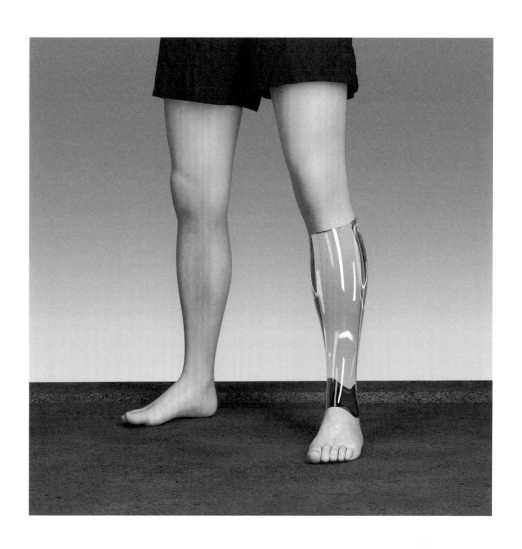

Hyperdressing: Wearable Technology in the Time of Global Warming
Susan Elizabeth Ryan

My title is inspired by the writings of Timothy Morton. In several books, including *The Ecological Thought* (2010) and *Hyperobjects* (2013), Morton writes that hyperobjects are giant physical and social systems that engulf us but cannot be completely perceived – like global warming or capitalism. We (humans) are objects among countless numbers of objects, some material and some not, comprising meshes of phenomena and relations that impinge upon us.[1] My use of the term 'hyperdressing', in light of Morton's ideas, is (admittedly) hyperbole – somewhat metaphorical, but based on the fact that dressing in any era comprises beliefs, behaviours and a vast range of objects and technologies arrayed on our bodies that administer to our human condition. I hope to show that our dressing behaviour is shifting from the fashion paradigm, expressing individual self-identity, to a next phase: clothing and equipping a 'no-self', a condition of far greater intimacy with the vast array of objects (including what we archaically call beings). This state of intimacy within interobjectivity is illustrated for Morton by the photographer Judy Natal's *Future Perfect: Steam Portrait #28*, about which he writes, 'The uncanny nothingness of the cloud forces the viewer into a disturbing intimacy with the clothed figure'. The role of technologies that are worn on the body, and our emerging awareness of such 'disturbing intimacies', is the subject of this essay.

Although the total gestalt of hyperobjects is by definition not perceptible due to their expansiveness and pervasiveness, they become visible in traumatic events and measurable changes that take place over time. In the case of dressing (behaviour that responds to the relations, or perceived relations, between our bodies and other 'objects' in our environment), there are two drivers of accelerating change:

1
Dressing's historical ability to absorb and embody technologies – and now its role in the race towards wearable technologies; and

2
The escalating awareness of physical peril (real or perceived) brought about by ecological and environmental realities.

Dress and Technology

In my study of dress and technology, *Garments of Paradise: Wearable Discourse in the Digital Age*, I argue that historians and archaeologists have always considered garments to be among the technological advancements of civilizations since ancient times.[2] Simply put, dress is technology: it absorbs the latest discoveries and incorporates ever better solutions for our physical and psychological needs. Part of the technological 'boundupedness' of dress is its ability to manifest our cravings for physical enhancement, to launch abilities beyond our bodies.

Historically, from providing warmth and advantages in battle to facilitating sexual reproduction and social selection, technologies have adapted to our bodies to allow us to become (or imagine becoming) more agile and powerful, more sexual and desirable (e.g. the attention to sleekness was aided by the development of synthetic fibres in the early twentieth century), or more or less noticeable. During the first half of the last century, driven by two world wars and the rhetoric of eugenics, our popular imaginations were filled with powerfully dressed superheroes, often with garments or gadgets enabling enhanced strength, vision, speed, even the ability to fly (e.g. the adornments of superheroes from Batman to Green Lantern). The actual technologies to bring about such fantasies would be generated by the electronic devices developed only after World War II, with strides in computing power and miniaturization. For example, the SONY Walkman, introduced in 1979, spawned generations of mobile (wearable) entertainment products. By the end of the last century, we explored the fantasy of merging with machines: bionic superheroes, fictional cyborgs. And the first actual wearable computers appeared.

Those began to be developed in the 1990s at centres such as the MIT Media Lab, Carnegie Mellon and Georgia Tech in the US. The early, geeky, hard-box wearable computers were complicated and expensive, and start-up companies such as Charmed Technologies, which tried to forge a market for them by presenting them as fashion, had an uphill climb. As Maggie Orth, wearable-technology designer and founder of International Fashion Machines observed, clothing lines in the Nineties were interested in garments that lit up or responded to the wearer with functioning electronics. Once a module was tooled, hundreds of thousands had to be sold to create a profit, whereas clothing producers projected on a scale of tens of thousands of units because of the scope and rapid turnover of the fashion industry. One popular wearable tech (henceforth, WT) item in the Nineties was LA Gear's Lights sneakers. With LEDs in the heels that flashed with the pressure of heel

Judy Natal's *Future Perfect* photographic series explores three evocative sites: a Las Vegas desert preserve; research facility Biosphere 2's experimental tracts in Oracle, Arizona; and Iceland's geothermal landscapes, where human intervention and land use are questioning the quality and state of futurity.

Susan Elizabeth Ryan

strikes, the Lights sold over five million pairs and became iconic, if isolated, evidence of industry's aspirations for WT. But aspirations outraced abilities. Breakthroughs for marketable WT came slowly, and were rarely adopted by mainstream dressing. Despite many campaigns for WT products, only illuminated garments received much attention. 2008–10 were banner years for LED couture, a short-lived 'red carpet' trend in the midst of the economic downturn. But with the rise of social media accessed through mobile phones, in the past few years it has been devices rather than garments that have achieved sophisticated design and display, in tune with digital capitalism. Watches and other wearables, most notably Google's ill-fated Glass, have sought to leverage the accomplishments of handheld phones and their systems to mete out the enhancements we crave – instantaneous memory access, communication and security (albeit in the form of surveillance). And there has been steady growth in health monitoring systems – long strapped on to bodies in the medical environment, but now walking the streets. In the 2010s, Fitbits and related devices have become accessories of choice, by which we constantly measure our personal progress or decline.

Our sleek new devices now take on the very issue of dress itself. If, as Orth points out, wearable electronics are far more instrumentalized than fashionable dress, then they support a more computational and socially monitored perception of ourselves than does traditional fashion that changes season-by-season. So, is the very notion of dress itself changing as we relate more mechanically and virtually to the world and each other? Will we witness something akin to the literary and social utopian dress posited by early modernism? Vladimir Tatlin's unisex worker's clothing, or the uniforms of so many modernist visions, from Alexander Bogdanov's sci-fi novel *Red Star* (1908), about a socialist utopia on Mars, to George Orwell's *1984* (1934) and even Mao Zedong's Chinese Cultural Revolution (beginning in 1966) – all of which advocated functional universal dress. These were often blocky suits or overalls, with little or no individual variation. In support of this, some point to the recent rise of 'normcore' – bland, anti-fashion attire – the latest trend for plain, traditional clothes that fade into the background as we focus on our devices. In the Google/Apple version of future dress, our sleekly designed enhancements signal that individuality is inside, or invisible, or dispersed across a wider net. Our bodies and social lives are endlessly attended to, but will our reliance on walk-in closets fade away? As early as 1964, Marshall McLuhan suggested that societies developing electronic media would adopt nudity – might he be right after all?[3]

Body

The Climate Dress designed in 2009 by Diffus, Hanne-Louise Johannesen and Michel Guglielmi uses conductive thread embroidery, LilyPad Arduino, sensors and LEDs to detect high CO2 ambient pollution levels.

Dress, Technology and Environmental Impact

So far, the fashion industry is in no danger; it adapts. In the twenty-first century, under accelerated post-industrial capitalism and aided by markets' increasing ability to exploit dress's psychological potential through brand imaging and social media (YouTube video and blog posts by 'beauty gurus'), we have fast fashion – cheap, outsourced gobs of garments with incredibly rapid obsolescence. The term 'landfill fashion' refers to the trendy, low-cost garments of certain fashion chains serving consumers with shrinking attention spans facing an increasing vastness of choices, and sourced from expanding factories in China and Vietnam – and Bangladesh, until the appalling factory collapse in 2013.[4] Mountains of cast-off clothes pass to thrift stores and are carted to post-consumer sorting facilities, where about thirty per cent of it is recycled and the rest baled for export to developing nations. Most of it becomes garbage, contributing to escalating dumpsites and 'trash islands' in nearly every ocean. The presence of toxic chemicals, fire retardants, dyes made of heavy metals, and petroleum and other toxic processing agents in synthetic fibres make this trash lethal.

By the same token, the amount of electronic devices and components, increasing exponentially in accordance with Moore's Law, is also creating vast piles of garbage. According to the US Environmental Protection Agency, in 2000, 4.6 million tons of e-waste – discarded electronics and components, which include toxic chemicals that leach into land over time or are released into the atmosphere – ended up in landfills in the US. CBS News reported in 2013 that fifty million tons of e-waste per year were sent to dumps. A United Nations study estimated that e-waste would grow from 48.9 million metric tons worldwide in 2012 to more than sixty-six million metric tons in 2017. The predictions may be imprecise, but by all accounts the amounts are astronomical.[5]

As we consider the potential expansion of WT mobile devices, based on the heated market in the past few years, we might imagine two enormous flows of toxic trash converging. E-textiles, including nanoparticle-coated fibres, present upwardly scaling challenges that we have barely begun to study. As fashion-based WT grows, we can project a situation that compares figuratively with Walter Benjamin's image of the 'Angel of History' (based on Paul Klee's 1920 painting, *Angelus Novus*):

[The angel's] eyes are staring, his mouth is open, his wings are spread. This is how one pictures the angel of history. His face is turned towards the past. Where we perceive a chain of events, he sees one single catastrophe which keeps piling wreckage upon

Susan Elizabeth Ryan

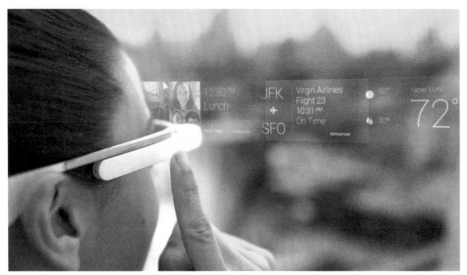

Google Glass interface simulating view of data 'timeline', overlaid on normal view as introduced in 2013 on a tutorial video

wreckage ... A storm is blowing from Paradise ... The storm irresistibly propels him into the future to which his back is turned, while the pile of debris before him grows skyward. This storm is what we call progress.[6]

But now the piles of debris are real, not imagery – they are toxic, and the angel is us.

Invisible Computing and WT

The backward vision presented by Benjamin also portrays our flawed perception of a situation beyond our reach. Timothy Morton describes this as the ontological asymmetry between humans and non-humans in a time of hyperobjects. Global warming (Morton rejects the polite term, climate change) already engulfs us – we cannot recycle our way out of it: 'we discover that the space we inhabit is not open and neutral, but is the interior of a gigantic iceberg whose seeming transparency was simply a matter of our less than adequate eyes. Flying through the universe in the space shuttle of modernity ... we have woken up inside an object, like a movie about being buried alive.'[7] Our eyes are already asymmetrical with our bodies, which are entangled with the world of objects.

As an iconic example of WT (or at least, a great creator of 'buzz'), Google's Glass forms a case study of how we seek to control and manipulate our vision. A culmination of techno dreams of physical and mental enhancements, Glass offered us immediacy of information access and communication, and power over our physical contexts via its camera and GPS – all packaged in a heads-up, hands-free accessory that could imitate glasses or accommodate the most stylish frames. Of course, power works both ways, and alongside the privacy concerns that were raised by many, there were possible health and environmental hazards from Glass's microwave emissions, and impacts on vision such as binocular rivalry; visual interference; and phoria, a misalignment occurring when both eyes are not looking at the same thing.[8] But Glass also fictionalizes reality by asserting that we are in control of all we see. The chaos of the world is reorganized through the data overlay. Why fear climate change when we can call up statistical forecasts and chart a safe course? As Morton says, it is not as easy as that: 'The more data we have about hyperobjects the less we know.'[9]

Like almost all the prototypes for industrially produced WT today, Glass was built on the assumptions of ubiquitous computing, a term coined by Mark Weiser in the 1980s. Weiser's fundamental principle was technology's drive to disappear. In a talk given

The 'Human Sensor' project by media artist Kasia Molga proposes hi-tech illuminated costumes and masks, exploring air pollution and the effect it has on human beings.

at Xerox PARC in 1994, he said, 'Good technology is invisible … ubiquitous computing is about "invisible" computing.'[10] Weiser envisioned ubiquitous technology (ubicomp) as augmentation, a way of being in the world, and the opposite of virtual reality, which involved withdrawal from the world. He imagined ubiquitous technology as the natural and empowered response to the overwhelming realities around us, releasing us from the stresses of information overload. It would calm us down, he said.

Weiser was a thoughtful techno-scientist, but his early death in 1999 prevented the evolution of his ideas and any reassessments he might have made as technologies advanced. Instead of being improved or re-evaluated, Weiser's calm world of augmented reality became the norm for developers. In 1997, Rosalind Picard formulated 'affective computing', whereby devices that read our biometrics activate on our behalf, allowing computers to become more invisible still, operating autonomously all around us. Since then, most technology that interfaces with our bodies has sought this holy grail of 'intuitiveness' by making the computational interface function like a seamless part of us, such that we are invisibly enhanced and at the centre of our world. That model of invisible control trades on our age-old desire to leap beyond the limitations of our bodies and effortlessly navigate our complex environments free of stress.

But, as Morton points out, the very notion of our 'world' is itself a concept that we create and believe in. Our belief is 'a token, a mental object that you grip as hard as possible, like your wallet or your keys'. Nothing is more manufactured than the smooth, controllable data flows that Glass, or even our smartphones, offer as part of our personal vision. Nevertheless, the very scale of what we experience at this time – extreme weather, Big Data and violent social upheavals – means that cracks in our world view, no matter how much it might be enhanced, arise with increasing frequency. Morton writes, 'World is a fragile aesthetic effect whose corners we are beginning to see.'[11]

Capitalism and the 'Empire of Fashion'
It is clear that the dynamics between bodies and environments are changing. And that includes fashion, the dominant dressing paradigm since the Industrial Revolution. Fashion is the essential expression of modern, democratic societies. What French social philosopher Gilles Lipovetsky called the 'Empire of Fashion' (in 1987) operated at the level of civic behaviour. He argued that mass-produced fashion offers nuances of choice and symbolism, which in turn enable consumers to behave as complex individuals

Susan Elizabeth Ryan

Fitbit is one of the most popular wearable-technology devices for fitness tracking, to measure data such as the number of steps walked, heart rate, quality of sleep, steps climbed and other personal metrics.

Tikker is a wristwatch designed by Fredrik Colting that counts down to the date of your death based on data such as age, BMI or where its users live, and comparing them to the average life expectancy of people in their demographic.

within democratic societies: 'Fashion is one of the faces of modern artifice, of the effort of human beings to make themselves masters of the conditions of their own existence.'[12]

In the 1990s, Lipovetsky updated the text, adding that the 'logic of appearances' had moved from dress to the body, and prestige based on distinctions of dress was ebbing in favour of skin-based display including tattoos, body-building regimens and plastic surgery. Today, body-based enhancements coordinate with the growing interest in health-monitoring systems and in the self as a physical project – monitoring will improve our exercise, weight loss and sleep habits in a never-ending process of perpetual training, what Gilles Deleuze placed at the heart of what he calls 'Societies of Control'.[13] In fact, we acquiesce to these never-ending programming and retraining regimens in continuous cycles of self-improvement that are never complete but must be constantly maintained.

Quantified Self vs. 'No-self'
The WT industry has leveraged itself on our intense fixation with ourselves as bundles of flesh and functions that are increasingly monitored and measured, a movement termed the 'Quantified Self' (QS) by Gary Wolf in 2007.[14] The proliferation of health-monitoring devices drives expectations for WT. In 2013, Forbes predicted that 2014 would be the 'Year of the Wearable', and a year later Gartner Market Research reported that personal health and fitness devices would be a five billion dollar market by 2016.[15] The problem is, the more data we generate about ourselves, the more data we encounter – and the larger the task of maintaining systems, training plans and upgrades, all seeming to manifest a control society beyond even Deleuze's wildest dreams.

If this trend continues, it seems likely that devices will eventually challenge our notion of dress as based on making choices (Lipovetsky), and move towards a different paradigm based on analyzing biometrics. And the possibilities are expanding. Already, a macabre chronometer watch called Tikker, from a start-up company crowdfunded in 2013, calculates its wearer's life expectancy and proceeds to count down to her projected time of death. *Carpe diem!*

Some, like Dawn Nafus and Jamie Sherman, view the emergence of the QS-driver-of-wearable-devices as a dialectical response to universal corporate control represented by Big Data. They write that self-monitoring via wearable biometric devices, while still part of the reach of Big Data, constitutes a 'soft resistance' by which individuals retain the possibility to evaluate the data

Japanese artist Atsuko Tanaka wearing her piece Electric Dress, during a performance and exhibition in 1956 organized by the Gutai group, an avant-garde artists' movement to which she belonged until 1965.

they receive and choose how they deploy it. While the algorithms of our devices analyse data according to corporate categories and the marketing goals behind them, users work through 'the constant unfolding of meaning to critically question what constitutes relevant information, whether individual datapoints or entire categories of information'. But in the end, the independence of the user is limited, and Nafus and Sherman concede that 'self-trackers are making a lateral move', working both beyond and within received categories.[16] Even a wearable like Glass, which attempted to control the intersection between biometrics and Big Data, offered a framed experience, one always pointed towards us. That is what customizing algorithms do. Glass 'fits' Big Data to us, just as fitness bands and health devices put us at the centre of data and 'tailor' it to us. It is the new technological sartorial, fitted to our desires – the ultimate custom couture.

Morton talks about our frequent encounters with massive amounts of data as an indicator that we – humans – are becoming more aware of hyperobjects. And we are becoming aware of our inability to truly measure them due to their vastness in time and space and their ability to both 'stick to' us and, at the same time, withdraw. Global warming is like that, and so is Big Data. Data sticks to us through our wearable devices, yet we can never finally grasp it all. We deal with ever greater scales of things. For Morton, what is occurring is 'the gradual realization by humans that they are not running the show, at the very moment of their most powerful technical mastery on a planetary scale'.[17] Morton points to possibilities other than mastery. He references the philosopher Derek Parfit's idea of 'no-self': 'a liberating abandonment of dominating self-interest'. Parfit writes, '[Before,] I seemed imprisoned in myself … I now live in the open air. There is still a difference between my life and the lives of other people, but that difference is less. Other people are closer. I am less concerned about the rest of my own life and more concerned about the lives of others.'[18] This 'no-self' is not self-obliteration and not dehumanization (as the Quantified Self appears to be) but a 'radical encounter with intimacy'. Unlike Tikker, which tracks our progress towards death, hyperobjects force a closeness with mortality, with other beings and objects, and with the unknowable. And according to Morton, 'Intimacy and the no-self view come together in ecological awareness.'[19]

One means of becoming open to the reality of our condition might be via aesthetics – actually a particular aesthetic that Morton characterizes as demonic or uncanny. This aesthetic incorporates the 'terrifying glimpse' of, say, ghosts: 'a glimpse that makes one's physicality resonate' – and he references Theodor

Susan Elizabeth Ryan

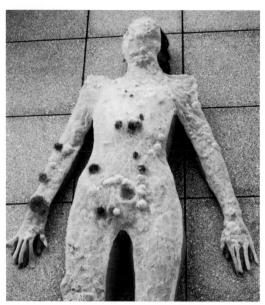

'The Textured Self' is a speculative project by designer Sonja Bäumel that takes inspiration from bacteria taken from the artist's own body to create hand-knitted and crocheted human-shaped silhouettes.

Adorno's comment that the primordial aesthetic experience is goosebumps.[20] This physical glimpse supports a sense of intimacy, even of being 'too close' to other life and other objects – and to the life in other objects.

I will always remember an early childhood nightmare from which I awoke in a sweat. In the dream, a familiar floor lamp with a bare electrical bulb moved towards me in my bedroom. It reminds me of some early artistic uses of wearable technology, such as Atsuko Tanaka's *Electric Dress* (1956), which appeared as a giant pile of light bulbs, replete with tangled wiring, moving towards the audience in the performance space. The bizarreness of the experience was felt even more by the artist who wore the 'dress' and contemplated electrocution. Tanaka told an interviewer, 'I had a fleeting thought, is this how a death-row inmate would feel?'[21]

Feeling unsafe around technology is a feature of our embeddedness in a world of forces that we try to push into the background. The 'uncanny' brings about both an aesthetic closeness (not aesthetic distance) and an openness that Morton calls rest. Rest is an aesthetic event reflected in Tanaka's work. Rest-as-aesthetic includes (according to Morton) shock, stunned silence and an attunement to the not-human. If we compare Morton's concept of 'rest' with Mark Weiser's notion of 'calm' (as in 'calm technology'), which has been the driving conceptual premise behind capitalist technological evolution, we discover that the two notions – linguistically so close – are really opposites. Weiser's calm technology referred to the fact that when we focus on anything – driving a car is the example that he used – we also notice things that happen on the periphery, like a child playing in the passenger seat. True calmness involves effective mastery of the interaction between focus and periphery, in order to achieve a sense of locatedness. For Weiser, the job for a useful technology is to master centre / periphery such that users remain aware, but can focus on what they want: 'As we learn to design calm technology, we will enrich not only our space of artifacts, but also our opportunities for being with other people. Thus may design of calm technology come to play a central role in a more humanly empowered twenty-first century.'[22]

But since Weiser wrote that in 1995, technology design has changed. First, interaction is increasingly treated not as something to be eradicated but rather as a sensually appealing experience.[23] Second, this experience has expanded opportunities for 'brandedness' and more sophisticated tools, which direct users' actions more effectively, rather than (as Weiser envisioned) enhancing user awareness. Simon Penny notes the recent development of ubiquitous computing on two fronts:

Body

1

the still invisible, 'clandestine, faceless technologies that involve distributed units in a larger control array …'; and

2

'garrulous, clingy technologies close to the body' – encompassing WT that has commercially come of age.

Penny finds neither of these trends particularly calming: 'how far have we come … is the automated processing of logical operations necessarily applicable and an asset in every aspect of life?'[24]

On the other hand, rest or restfulness within the context of hyperobjects is not about human empowerment, or directing perception, but just the opposite.

Our bodies exist in a world of things – meshes of things – that we cannot control or even recognize, but which none the less transform us. It is like jumping into a pool of cold water. The mind-cancelling physical shock subsides and we acclimatize to entirely new conditions and possibilities: drowning, but also floating. We could be terrified, or we could rest and allow ourselves to be buoyed up. This is the aesthetic response. In her research project, *Fifty Percent Human*, textile artist Sonja Bäumel works with the fact that half the cells in our body are not our cells ('ourselves') but microbes ('others'). In the piece *The Textured Self* (2011), she produced a hand-crocheted interpretation of, as she writes, a 'bacteria membrane consisting of individual skin bacteria and the ones of the environment of one day'.[25] This invites the restful intimacy of the too-close.

'Hyperobjects' is, of course, not a technical term – but for Morton, it is applicable to the technological age, which is also the age of global warming and events and objects that overwhelm us. The 'rest' that he refers to is not safe, and does not provide the illusion of security but rather the acceptance of coexistence. He cites John Keats, who wrote about the poet as a spirit that has no self, but absorbs everything around him – Keats called himself a 'Camelion [sic] Poet'.[26] If we are one day overcome by environmental trauma, or, for whatever reason, we find ourselves catapulted beyond our capitalist behaviour and reliance on technologies of control, then perhaps our future dressing might become a hyperdressing. It would involve accepting our asymmetrical existence and, chameleon-like, becoming intimate in the time of hyperobjects.

1 Timothy Morton, *Hyperobjects: Philosophy and Ecology After the End of the World* (Minneapolis, MN, 2013); Morton, *The Ecological Thought* (Cambridge, MA, 2010).

2 Susan Elizabeth Ryan, *Garments of Paradise: Wearable Discourse in the Digital Age* (Cambridge, MA, 2014), pp.17–19.

3 Marshall McLuhan, 'Clothing: Our Extended Skin' in McLuhan, *Understanding Media: The Extensions of Man* (Cambridge, MA, 1994), p.121. (Original publication, 1964.)

4 Jim Zarroli, 'In the Trendy World of Fast Fashion, Styles Aren't Made to Last', *NPR News* (March 11, 2013). See also Syed Zain Al-Mahmood, Christina Passariello and Preetika Rana, 'The Global Garment Trail: From Bangladesh to a Mall Near You', *Wall Street Journal* (May 3, 2013).

5 Greenpeace International, 'Where does e-waste end up?' (February 24, 2009); Shoshana Davis, 'E-Waste: What Happens with Your Outdated or Broken Gadgets', *CBS News Online* (April 22, 2013); United Nations University, 'StEP Launches Interactive World E-Waste Map', press release (December 16, 2012)

6 Walter Benjamin, 'Theses on the Philosophy of History' in Benjamin, *Illuminations*, translated by Harry Zohn (London, 1973), pp.259–60.

7 Morton, *Hyperobjects*, p.160.

8 See, for example, Joel M. Moskowitz, 'Google Glass Radiation: Health Risk from Wearable Wireless Smartphones', *RFSafe* (April 15, 2014); Alise Ackerman, 'Could Google Glass Hurt Your Eyes?' *Forbes Online* (March 4, 2013).

9 Morton, *Hyperobjects*, p.180.

10 Mark Weiser, 'Building Invisible Interfaces', talk at Computer Science Lab, Xerox PARC, Palo Alto, CA (November 2, 1994); Weiser, 'The Computer for the Twenty-First Century', *Scientific American* (September 1991), pp.94–100.

11 Morton, *Hyperobjects*, pp.99–100.

12 Gilles Lipovetsky, The *Empire of Fashion*: Dressing *Modern Democracy*, translated by Catherine Porter (Princeton, NJ, 1994), pp.24 and 243.

13 Gilles Deleuze, 'Postscript on Societies of Control' in *The Cybercities Reader*, ed. Stephen Graham (New York, 2004), p.75. (Original publication, 1988.).

14 Gary Wolf, 'Quantified Self', *Wired* (2007).

15 Ewan Spence, '2014 Will Be the Year of Wearable Technology', *Forbes Online* (November 2, 2013); Gartner's report was cited in Keith Wagstaff, 'Data Overload: Is the "Quantified Self" Really the Future?' *NBC News Online* (August 30, 2014).

16 Dawn Nafus and Jamie Sherman, 'This One Does Not Go Up To Eleven: The Quantified Self Movement as an Alternative Big Data Practice', *International Journal of Communication* 8 (2014), 8.

17 Morton, *Hyperobjects*, p.164.

18 Morton, *Hyperopbjects*, pp.138–9, quoting from Derek Parfit, *Reasons and Persons* (Oxford, 1984), 281.

19 Morton, *Hyperobjects*, p.139.

20 Morton, *Hyperobjects*, p.169. Reference is from Theodor Adorno, *Aesthetic Theory*, translated and edited by Robert Hullot-Kentor (Minneapolis, MN, 1997), p.331.

21 Tanaka quoted in Ming Tiampo, 'Electrifying Painting' in *Electrifying Art: Atsuko Tanaka 1954-1968*, eds. Mizuho Kato and Ming Tiampo (New York, 2004), p.72.

22 Mark Weiser and John Seely Brown, 'Designing Calm Technology', (December 21, 1995). See also Mark Weiser and John Seely Brown, 'The Coming Age of Calm Technology (October 5, 1996, quoted in Mark B. N. Hansen, 'Ubiquitous Sensation: Toward an Atmospheric, Collective, and Microtemporal Model of Media' in Throughout: Art and Culture Emerging with Ubiquitous Computing, ed. Ulrik Ekman (Cambridge, MA, 2013), p.67.

23 Lev Manovich, 'Interaction as Designed Experience' in *Throughout*, pp.312–13.

24 Simon Penny, 'Trying To Be Calm: Ubiquity, Cognitivism, and Embodiment' in *Throughout*, p.268.

25 See Sonja Bäumel's artist's website.

26 Morton, *Hyperobjects*, pp.197–8.

Hussein Chalayan
Room Tone

Hussein Chalayan MBE was born in Nicosia, Cyprus and educated both in Cyprus and England. After graduating from Central Saint Martins with a BA (Hons) degree in Fashion in 1993, Chalayan formed his own fashion house showcasing his twice-yearly collections in highly curated shows that engaged with politically, socially and technologically challenging subjects. He has twice been named British Designer of the Year – in 1999 and 2000 – and received an MBE in the Queen's Birthday Honours List in 2006. He is design consultant to Parisian heritage brand Vionnet, and is the head professor of the fashion department at the University of Applied Arts in Vienna.

One Hundred and Eleven, Spring/Summer collection, 2007

LED dress featuring electronics by Moritz Waldemeyer and Swarovski crystals, Autumn/Winter collection, 2007

After Words, Autumn/Winter collection, 2000, featuring the Coffee Table Dress

'Room Tone' is a response to the nature of London life. It consists of a series of studies of emotional states that characterize different aspects of living in this city. They reflect certain attitudes or realities, including our remoteness from nature, the way we repress our emotions and the idea that the city is a place of potential danger. Each one is both a reaction to and a proposal for how London life can be experienced.

The project was originally conceived as an alternative concept for a catwalk show in which, rather than merely presenting a surface reality – clothing – one could also make inner states visible. The evolution of wearable technology has meant that it is already routine for people to measure their heart rates, sleeping patterns and fitness. But by tracking these biological rhythms differently, it should be possible to capture emotional states and for these inner realities to be revealed.

This project aims to do that through two wearable devices developed in collaboration with the microchip maker Intel. We have developed a pair of sunglasses designed to capture the wearer's brain activity, pulse and breathing rhythm. That combination of data – captured through tiny sensors embedded in the frame – should provide a picture of the wearer's stress response to a given situation. Meanwhile, the sunglasses will transmit the data by Bluetooth to a belt embedded with a projector, which projects images reflecting the wearer's state of mind.

For the fashion show, the idea was to have five models each wearing this pair of devices, and each putting a particular emotion on display. Before their turn on the runway, each model would be primed with a set of images selected to trigger or arouse a particular emotion. As part of the performance, their response would be projected on a wall as they walk. At the same time, they will be briefed to try to control their response by controlling their breathing, which will influence the nature of the images projected on the wall. So the performance is designed to elicit a reaction, which is put on display, and an attempt to control that reaction, which is also visible.

The five themes, or emotional states, to be explored are as follows:

Outer Measure
Our increasing distance from nature, at least in urban life, creates an urge to immerse ourselves in nature – visually, physically and mentally. In this scenario, the wearer meditates on imagery of flowers, taking the time to focus on their qualities and connect with them mentally. The eyewear measures brain activity and heartbeat, while the bridge of the spectacles measures breath. This data affects an image of roses projected from the belt: a measuring scale, such as you might see in the optical sight of a rifle, hovers over the image, measuring the model's concentration and focus. It shifts around, depending on how still the model can keep it with their breath – all of which is displayed on the image projected on the wall as the model walks.

Beings
For most of us, sexual fantasies are private, taboo, something unspoken.

Here, the interactive accessories record the wearer's reaction to imagery of sexual fantasies, potentially enabling a person to express desires without having to speak them. In this case, the wearer is primed with imagery of sexual activity and their reaction is displayed on the image projected on the wall. The background is an animated scene of tangled bodies, on which the appearance of black pixels reflects the wearer's heart rate while pink pixels reflect brain activity. The faster the heartbeat, the more black pixels appear, while the more brain activity there is the more pink pixels appear. Both sets of pixels can be controlled using the breath.

Stiff Upper Lip
The difficulty of expressing emotions remains a distinct feature of British culture despite the exposure to so many other cultures in modern British life. In 'Stiff Upper Lip', an image of a rose is partially concealed by a coloured square. The more emotion the glasses detect, the more of the rose is visible. But the higher the stress level, the more the emotions are being repressed – and thus, the more the square will conceal the rose.

Imminence of Danger
Fear of terrorism has become part of daily life in the UK and many other countries. One might describe it as an 'asymmetrical world war', in which the danger is invisible and yet, if you read the newspapers, it feels as though it can materialize anywhere, anytime. In this theme, the belt projects an image of a public space with people walking across it. The higher the heartbeat and brain activity, the more the space fills up with running legs. The lower the stress levels, the fewer legs traverse the space and the slower they walk.

Omnipresence
As a result of digital media and virtual reality, our experience of being in one place or another is becoming more and more indistinguishable. In 'Omnipresence', the accessories create an interplay between mind and body. The belt projects an image of a rope being pulled between two hands, symbolizing a low-tech connection between two bodies in two different parts of the world, each trying to keep the equilibrium along the length of the rope. In this case, the more stress or emotion detected by the eyewear, the more the pulling of the rope intensifies at one end rather than the other. By controlling the breath, the wearer can even out the forces across the rope and maintain the connection between the two bodies.

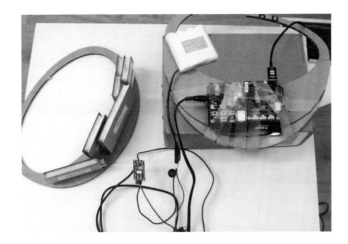

How to translate your state of mind into a performance: strap a projector around your waist. This is a prototype for a belt-projector that receives data from a pair of sunglasses (*overleaf*). The glasses pick up on brain activity, pulse and the rhythm of the wearer's breath through sensors in the arms and nose-piece.

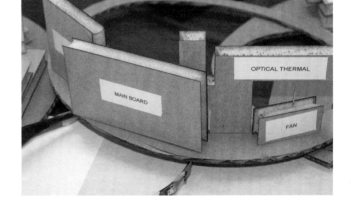

The belt, which receives signals via Bluetooth, has enough thickness to accommodate a compact projector. A later prototype (*overleaf*) conceals the projector in a relatively slender belt-pack.

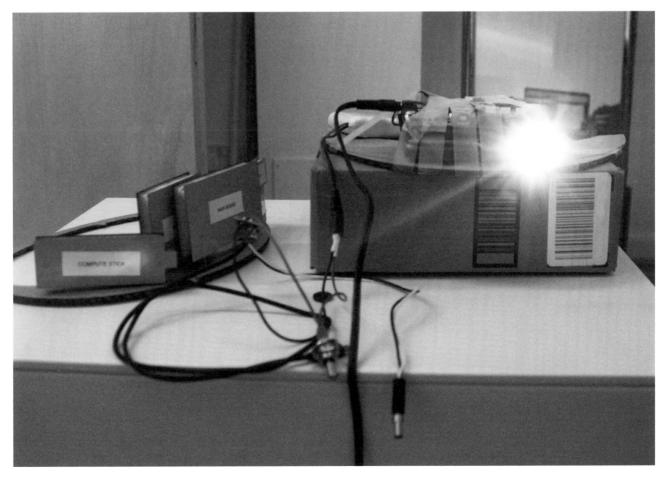

Hussein Chalayan

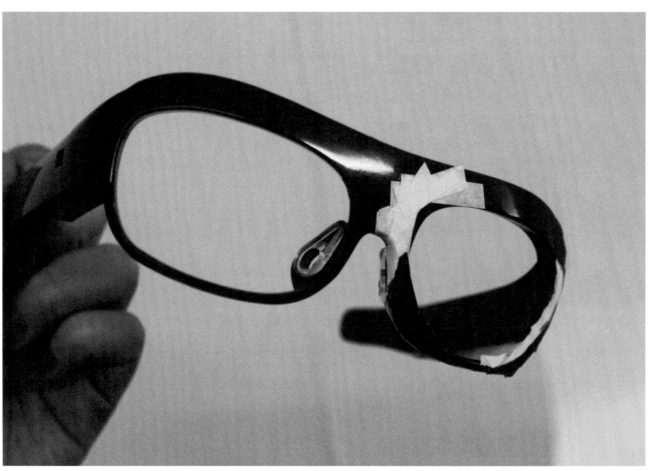

Hussein Chalayan

The very British concept of the stiff upper lip reflects a Victorian ideal in which the emotions are repressed. Here, that concept is represented by a rose being covered by a giant pixel, which grows depending on the wearer's state of agitation.

Hussein Chalayan in conversation with Justin McGuirk

JM HC

This project is about wearable technology. That's something that your work has addressed before, but this time you're focusing on emotional states.

I've done various things before, and also experimented with ideas that I didn't actually realize. So when we started collaborating with Intel, we had lots of ideas that have evolved over time. I think the essential thing I'm interested in is giving form to the intangible. A lot of my work is about that, somehow.

What's your attitude to wearables generally, or to the idea of putting sensors on the body? Do you have an optimistic take on these devices, or a more cynical one?

I'm generally cynical because often I don't like what I see with wearable technology. Often, it doesn't go with the body—it ignores the ways the body is structured, and denies its curves and movement. I also often find wearables very masculine. Whenever I work with technology for clothes, integration is always a big thing for me. When we made the dresses that moved from one era to another, for instance, everything was integrated into the corset, it wasn't just plonked on top. That is really important for me.

In this case, we're talking about quite standard-looking accessories. They don't announce themselves as 'wearable tech'.

Yes, it's a pair of sunglasses and a belt. The belt has a bit of thickness to it, because it has a projector built in. And the sensors are hidden in the glasses. It's all integrated—it's quite amazing. The sensors and the projector are connected via Bluetooth. So the eyewear does the sensing, and it informs the belt, which projects the image.

JM HC

What data are the devices sensing?

First of all, we're trying to record brain activity from two different sides of the brain, and we're connecting that with the heartbeat and the rhythm of the breath. We're treating the brain activity as a kind of natural state and using the breath as a control mechanism. So, in terms of what you'll experience, you will be primed by being shown certain material that, in theory, stimulates a reaction, and the belt will project images of your mental state on a wall. At that point, you will use your breath to try to influence the image, to calm your emotional state. We don't know how interactive it's going to be, or how much of the person's emotions the eyewear will detect, but it's a reciprocal experience—the person is both watching the images and reacting to them. In a way, it will be almost a meditative experience.

What emotional states are you hoping to capture?

Various ones: fear of terrorism, sexual desire, our alienation from nature. Also, there's the idea of not being able to express emotion, the idea of the 'stiff upper lip'. I'm representing that through the image of a flower that gets covered by a square pixel that gets bigger and smaller, covering up more or less of the flower. The symbols are getting purer and clearer as I develop this. And I like this way of working where I don't know what I'm going to end up with exactly, because it allows me and the people I work with to explore ideas.

Sometimes I feel that these ideas sound a lot grander than they are, and then you look at it and you think, 'Oh, was that it?' But your intention is still something. And the journey might be part of a broader process that leads to other ideas.

In many ways, what's actually being measured in each case is stress levels—is that right?

It's mostly about stress, but then also about how stress could be controlled by breathing. Because the minute that you breathe differently your stress levels can change. That's why they tell you, if you're stressed or having a panic attack, that you should breathe deeply.

You mentioned repressed emotions. How much are the states you're exploring a reflection on London life?

They are probably quite common in most northern European cities, but I'm interested in London because I think of it as the New York of Europe: as this state in itself. I'm a Londoner, but I'm from a Mediterranean background, so I am definitely part emotional and part cerebral. And while there are many positive things about living in London, I don't think it's emotionally super healthy—it's not a place where people express their emotions that well. I think that's why people here drink a lot. I come from a much more affectionate culture, which is also too much at times.

One of the emotions you're measuring is fear, and you specifically mention the fear associated with terrorism. If *Fear and Love* works as a title, it is partly because it picks up on a quality of the contemporary moment, including the presence of terrorism in the newspapers almost daily. Your project picks up on that.

If you draw a Venn diagram, the overlap is vulnerability. Love is a vulnerable state for me: quite a horrible thing in some ways, because it's painful to love. And fear is also painful. What I think they have in common is vulnerability.

I'm curious about how you see your work relating to issues in the world, because it clearly does. Do you find the freedom to do that because you have a slightly more artistic practice?

I think a lot of my work is definitely related to things that happen in the

world. I am an observer, and I am curious. So I like to connect my observations about things that are happening in the world with my design. For instance, the collection that is in our shops right now is all about Cuba. I made it about two years ago, before Cuba became a big topic. But I spent some time there and I sensed that this was a country of isolation, and I wanted to know what isolation breeds. Because I'm from an island as well, I know what it feels like. North Cyprus is not recognized internationally, but Greek Cyprus is. So I'm very aware of the nation state and what it means to be recognized, to actually live within your own means. What kind of mental state does that lead to? The project before that was based on the Orient Express, which looked at how the West exoticizes and orientalizes Istanbul. I think that a lot of my ideas revolve around my experience of the world. I guess I find ways in which I can explore them a bit more, absurd as it sounds, through clothes.

Do you see design changing as a profession?

Definitely, because digital media means that anyone can access anything—and it means also that there's no room to miss anything. I also think we're living in a world that is no longer about merit, but about who you know. In my opinion, nepotism is damaging creativity. And a lot of younger people … I don't know if they take risks as much as people did in the past. I think it's a less risk-taking society, at least in the creative world.

Is that because of the commercial pressures?

I think so. On the other hand, digital media has made everything more democratic. Anyone can design something and put it online, they don't have to rely on a buyer any more. You can communicate directly with your potential consumer. So that's exciting. It depends on how you use all this. It's like fire: you use it well, or you burn yourself with it—or you burn others with it.

Here, the rose represents nature, which city dwellers are so removed from. The more the wearer of the device can calm his or her mental activity and breath, the more the flower will come into focus.

Neri Oxman / Mediated Matter Group / Stratasys
Vespers: A Collection of Death Masks

Neri Oxman is an architect and designer based in Boston, Massachusetts. She is the Sony Corporation Career Development Professor and associate professor of Media Arts and Sciences at the MIT Media Lab, where she founded and directs the Mediated Matter design research group. Her work looks to nature for practical design solutions across scales, from the micro scale to the building scale, where technology and nature live in harmony. Oxman has been named in *Icon* magazine's list of the top twenty most influential architects to shape our future, and selected as one of the 100 most creative people by Fast Company.

Anthozoa, 3D-printed dress designed by Neri Oxman and Iris Van Herpen in collaboration wth Stratasys, 2012

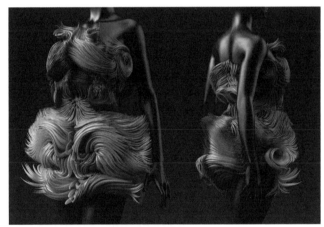

Zuhal, from the Wanderers collection, 2014

Björk wearing the Rottlace mask during a live performance at the Miraikan museum, Tokyo, 2016

Neri Oxman

D'où Venons Nous / Que Sommes Nous /
Où Allons Nous. [Where do we come from?
What are we? Where are we going?]
(Paul Gauguin)

Novel technologies are enabling design and production at nature's scale. We can seamlessly vary the physical properties of materials at the resolution of a sperm cell, a blood cell or a nerve cell. Stiffness, colour, transparency, conductivity, even smell and taste, can be individually tuned for each 3D pixel within a physical object. The generation of products is therefore no longer limited to assemblages of discrete parts made of homogeneous properties. Rather – like organs – objects can be composed of materials characterized by geometrical variation, material heterogeneity and multifunctionality.

Such technologies express the spirit of the age in design. Moreover, artefacts embody the tools and technologies used to design and make them. Some archetypes – such as automobiles, aeroplanes, garments, prosthetic devices and building skins – have evolved to improve the relationship between object, body and environment. Others have become relics. The subject of 'Vespers' is a relic: the death mask.

Traditionally made of a single material, such as wax or plaster, the death mask originated as a means of capturing a person's visage, keeping the deceased 'alive' through memory. The 'Vespers' death masks, however, are not intended to memorialize the dead. They are designed to reveal cultural heritage and speculate about the perpetuation of life, both cultural and biological. Unlike their traditional, handmade analogues, 'Vespers'' designs are *entirely* data driven, digitally generated, additively manufactured and, at times, biologically augmented. By pushing the boundaries of cusp technologies – such as high-resolution material modelling, multi-material 3D printing and synthetic biology – we explore the death mask's meaning and possible future utility, thus bringing it 'back to life'.

'Vespers' expresses the intertwining of fear and love through the continuity of death and life. Debuted in *Fear and Love*, it was created for *The New Ancient* collection, curated and manufactured by Stratasys Ltd. 'Vespers' masks five imaginary martyrs. Each martyr is memorialized at three different moments in human development: the past, the present and the future.

Series 1: Past, the 'Natural' World
Some of the most well-known death masks, like those of Agamemnon and King Tutankhamun, were either made entirely of, or inlaid with, precious stones and minerals. The use of colour often expressed the cultural attributes or spiritual powers of the deceased.

The first series explores life through the lens of death. It uses five colour combinations commonly found in religious and cultural practices across regions and eras. Each mask in this series is embedded with natural minerals, such as bismuth, silver and gold.

Colour combinations and the underlying geometry of the masks are driven by a parametric grammar. In this series, polyhedral meshes are 'evolved' into subdivided surfaces using an algorithm, which – like the formation of life itself – emulates cellular subdivision. Using a minimal set of rules, the series generates a plethora of shapes and their corresponding colours. The use of the Stratasys full-colour, multi-material 3D printing technology enables the creation of objects that have – for the first time in the history of additive manufacturing – the variety and nuance of ancient crafts.

Series 2: Present, the 'Digital' World
The custom of the death mask in the ancient world was believed to strengthen the spirit of the deceased and guard their soul from evil spirits on their way to the afterworld. In this view, death is a conduit to a form of rebirth. The mythical notion that the soul can be guided from a state of death to a new state of life inspired the masks in the second series. Here, we interpret the journey from death to life in a new way as we ask: can inner channels be designed that guide *real* micro-organisms? Can such channels 're-engineer' life and living?

The second series explores the transition between life and death: a metamorphosis. It moves beyond the exterior surface and into the interior volume of the mask. The inner structures are entirely data-driven, and are designed to match the resolution of microvasculature found in nature. Expressed through changes in form – from truncated to smoothly curved, from surface to volume modelling – this series conveys the sense of metamorphosis. Using spatial-mapping algorithms, we transformed the surface colorations in the first series into coloured, internal channels and conduits within transparent volumes. For example, the distribution of colours across the 'crown of thorns' of an imaginary martyr's first mask becomes a series of internal channels at the resolution of nerve axons.

In this series, it is the interplay of light that reveals the internal structures. Like spirits (from Latin *spiritus*, meaning 'breath'), these internal structures reference the distribution of the martyr's last breath. While internal vasculature can be designed to guide and control the biodegradation of life, can such inner structures be used, in the future, to guide and recreate life?

Series 3: Future, the 'Biological' World
What remains once life has been lived? Can the death mask drive the formation of new life forms? The third series revolves around death and rebirth, denoting both spiritual incarnation and biological recapitulation. In it, the masks become habitats for micro-organisms and the creation of new life.

While devoid of cultural expressions and nearly colourless, the masks in the third series are, ironically, the most alive: transitioning from a vessel of vasculature to what may become a biological urn. This return to life through nature marks a new cycle of life and the notion of continuation.

The masks in this series are populated with living micro-organisms, distributed according to the spatial logic provided by the second series. The micro-organisms and their by-products may recreate the colour palette of the first series, evoking those cultural associations. The martyrs' faces are no longer preserved but have transformed into sites of, and for, new life.

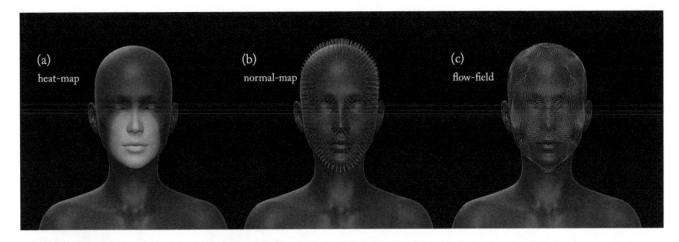

(a) heat-map (b) normal-map (c) flow-field

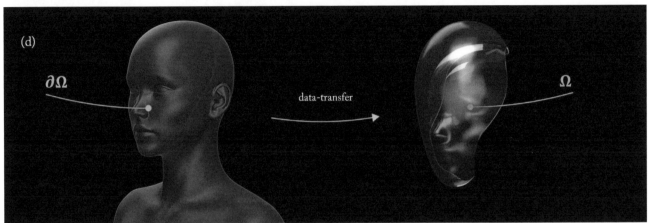

(d)

$\partial\Omega$ data-transfer Ω

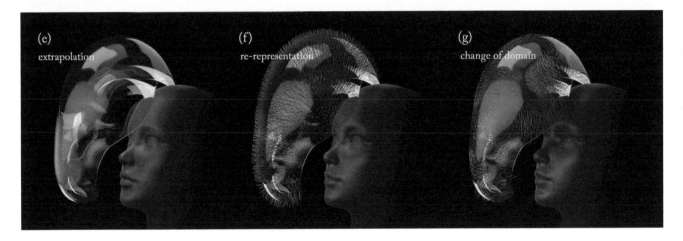

(e) extrapolation (f) re-representation (g) change of domain

Visualization of the design approach for Lazarus.
Its material composition is informed by the flow
of air and its distribution across the surface. Unlike
traditional death masks, the design of Lazarus is
entirely data driven and additively manufactured.
Data about the wearer's breath was captured (*above*)
through heat-mapping and velocity-testing and then
used to generate the form of the mask.

Neri Oxman

Three examples (*right*) of a data-driven material modelling approach, illustrating an array of internal compositions achieved through high-resolution deposition control of multiple materials.

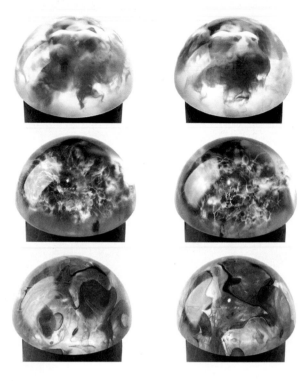

Side view and front view (*below and opposite*) of Mask 3 from Series 2. The internal composition is created through the aggregation and diffusion of vein-like structures informed by the geometric patterns of its predecessor mask in Series 1.

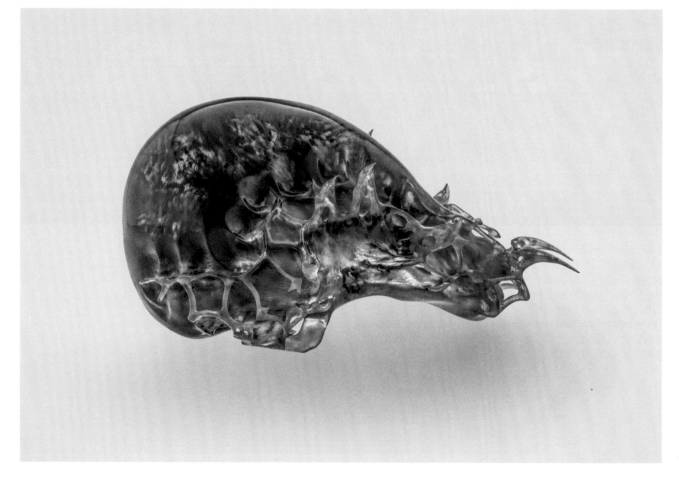

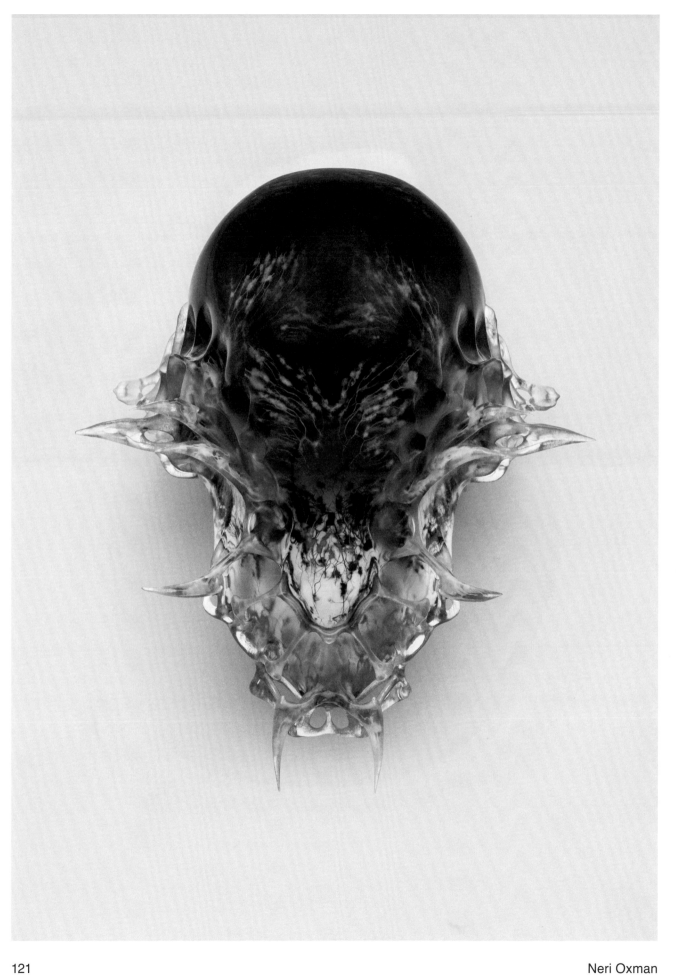

Body

Neri Oxman in conversation with Justin McGuirk

JM   NO

What led you to embark on
this body of work?

I have a long-standing collaboration with
the 3D printing company Stratasys Ltd,
and they asked me to contribute to a
collection they were producing called
The New Ancient. I wanted to revisit
the typology of the death mask. We were
intrigued by the idea of exploring an
ancient and long-forgotten 'product',
and giving it new meaning through design
technology. Especially exciting for us was
the challenge of transforming the customary
single-material mask, once moulded to the
face of the deceased and used as
memorabilia, into a multi-material multi-
functional mask.
　　'Vespers' is a natural extension
of previous works, such as 'Imaginary
Beings' and 'Wanderers'. In all three
collections, we explored a data-driven
approach to material modelling, where
both the geometry of an object and its
physical properties−such as rigidity,
opacity and colour−can be computer
generated. 'Vespers' is the most sophisticated expression of our design approach
so far, demonstrating that we can vary
the physical properties of materials in
extremely high resolution that matches,
and ultimately transcends, the scales
of nature.

How does it relate to the theme
of fear and love?

Oh, how doesn't it? Mark Twain once said
that the fear of death follows from the fear
of life; that a man who lives fully is pre-
pared to die at any time. As humans,
fear and love are the forces by which we
navigate both life and death. One cannot
exist without the other.
　　But also, the boundaries that distinguish life from death are vague and
complex. At times it is challenging to
determine where one ends and the other
begins. All living things are embedded
with death (think programmed cell death),
while the dead are teeming with life
(think of the complex ecosystem that
emerges soon after death, with decompo-
sition). Similarly, humanity's attempts to

JM   NO

understand death through tangible
expressions reveal the continuity
of human culture, which is−in itself
−the embodiment of life.

These are clearly artistic artefacts,
and yet you operate in a design and
technology context. What are the
practical applications of the techniques
you are using?

I don't consider the death masks artistic
artefacts but speculative design objects
demonstrating the use of novel, and
very real, technologies. I consider them
expressions of new forms of design.
Our research into high-resolution
multi-material modelling and bitmap 3D
printing is a good example. Our projects
require us to invent computational design
tools and technologies in order to create
them. We look for design opportunities
where the technique defines an expression as much as the expression defines
the technique. That's also how nature
works: bone for example−both its form
and formation process−adapts to the
load under which it's placed. Its density
varies as a function of the forces applied.
　　In terms of practical applications,
the first and second series in 'Vespers'
demonstrate the ability to design and
manufacture geometrically complex
and materially diverse objects. In nature,
we can observe that functionally graded
materials are vastly superior to assemblages. By varying material properties
within a single structure, you can minimize
the fracturing and damage where different
materials meet. That means you can
have stable objects that have different
properties: stiff and soft, or opaque and
transparent−objects that are multifunc-
tional. The ability to control and 'tune'
the properties of materials within a single
structure reduces the need for assem-
blies. This helps create sophisticated
behaviours in the design of biomedical
devices such as prosthetics and orthotics,
self-actuating soft-robotics, optics,
self-healing materials and highly custom-
ized building skins.
　　The third series in 'Vespers' explores
the interplay between the mask and the

living system it is designed to sustain. In this case, by varying the physical properties of the printed 'tissue' the mask guides biological growth. There are exciting practical applications with this approach, since designers are now able to control and pattern the growth of living systems through a computational algorithm. Consider photosynthetic wearables or buildings that generate biofuel. Combining computational design, additive manufacturing and synthetic biology, 'Vespers' points towards the far-reaching impact these technologies may have across seemingly disparate fields.

How near or far do you think these applications are from coming into their own?

Functionally graded products – or structures that are designed to vary their properties within a single object – are already coming into their own: prosthetic sockets and splints have variable elasticity, steel structural beams now have variable geometrical densities. The smaller you go in scale, the easier it appears to be to realize such opportunities. At the larger scale it's still harder to achieve variable-property additive manufacturing, but that will change – and so will the structural and environmental performance of buildings. Imagine the possibilities of designing entire building skins that operate like optical lenses, to filter light and temperature in and out of the building.

The body has always been a subject for design, but how much has it become a live material for design? In other words, are we getting to a point where any boundary between what is the natural body and what is a designed construct has become meaningless?

Yes! With recent advancements in digital fabrication, the scales of making, printing and building are approaching the already micro scales of mapping. Consider the ease with which you can transition from an MRI body scan of, say, a residual limb to a 3D print of a prosthetic device (with, by the way, 20 times the print resolution of the scan!). Or, consider the ability to 3D print synthetic wearable skins that not only contain biological media but can also filter such media in a selective manner. Imagine the possibility of 3D printing semipermeable walls, which can allow certain molecules or ions to pass through them. Given that today's Connex500 printers can 3D print at 16-micron resolution – hair-thickness resolution – it is possible to imagine designs where the channels inside a wearable skin contain micro-pores that can filter microbes and replenish the body. In this way, it is possible to imagine controlling the exchange of sucrose, biofuel and other nutrients between the wearable and the skin. These synthetic, liquid-containing garments could operate like the human skin, as both barrier and filter.

Designs that combine top-down form generation with the bottom-up growth of biological systems will open up real opportunities for designers working with digital fabrication and synthetic biology. Their main benefit is that they can create systems that are truly dynamic – products and building parts that can grow, heal and adapt. In the end, cells are just small self-replicating machines. If we can engineer them to perform useful tasks, simply by adding sugar and growth media, we can dream up new design possibilities.

Obviously death is our most fundamental fear as a species, but do you think society is anxious about the blurring of that boundary between biology and design? Or do you think this notion is overblown?

Just outside our lab space, at the [MIT] Media Lab, Kevin Esvelt is genetically engineering mice to save Nantucket from Lyme disease. Hugh Herr is designing wearable robotic human-machine interfaces to augment human locomotion. Ed Boyden is controlling neural functions using light for therapeutic applications. The notion is everything but overblown. It is, in fact, very real. The intersection of fields such as molecular biology, ecological engineering, robotics, design computation and additive manufacturing are constantly blurring the boundaries – between human and machine, and between natural and designed environments – to the point where such distinctions can no longer be made. They become entangled.

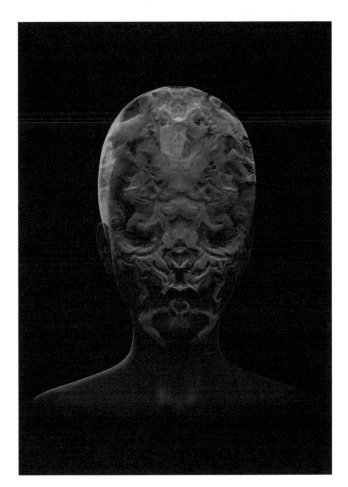 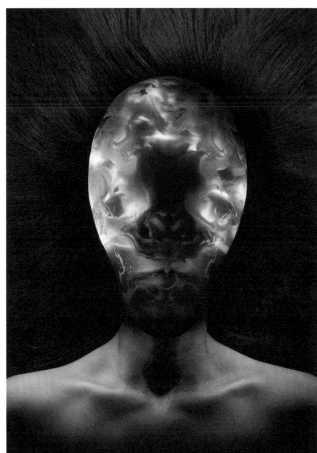

Lazarus is a 3D-printed wearable facial-cover designed to contain the wearer's last breath, serving as an "air urn" memento. The final mask (*right*) is shown against its 3D rendering.

Neri Oxman

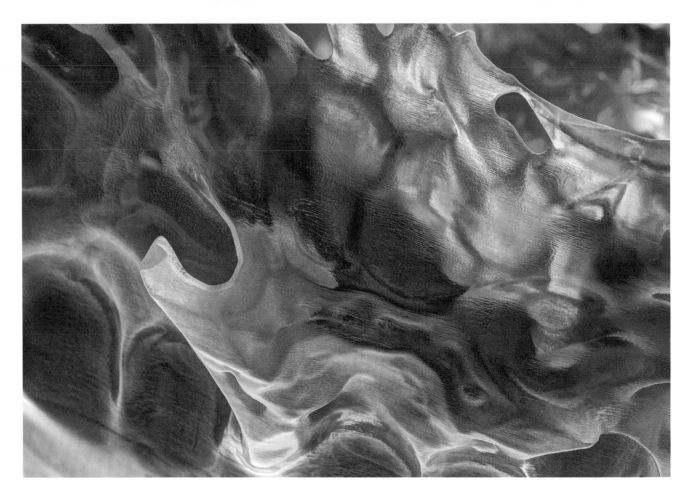

Close-up and front view (*opposite*) of Mask 1
from Series 2

Earth

From Oil Age to Soil Age
John Thackara

Why We Need a New Story

In 1971, a geologist called Earl Cook evaluated the amount of energy 'captured from the environment' in different economic systems. Cook discovered then that a modern city-dweller needed about 230,000 kilocalories per day to keep body and soul together. This compared starkly with a hunter-gatherer, 10,000 years earlier, who needed about 5,000 kcal per day to get by.[1]

That gap, between simple and complex lives, has widened at an accelerating rate since Cook's pioneering work. Once all the systems, networks and equipment of modern life are factored in—the cars, planes, factories, buildings, infrastructure, heating, cooling, lighting, food, water, hospitals, the internet of things, cloud computing—well, a New Yorker or Londoner today 'needs' about *sixty times* more energy and resources per person than a hunter-gatherer—and their appetite is growing by the day. To put it another way: modern citizens today use more energy and physical resources in a month than our great-grandparents used during their whole lifetime.[2]

It's a shame, in retrospect, that Earl Cook's easily grasped comparison was overshadowed by the publication of *Limits to Growth* a year later. That book, based on a computer model at MIT (Massachusetts Institute of Technology), warned of environmental 'overshoot and collapse' if the perpetual growth economy continued unchecked. The apocalyptic story in *Limits* generated plenty of fear—but it was also demoralizing. In the forty-five year stream of films, books and campaigns that followed its publication, the enormity of the challenges facing the planet contrasted starkly with the tiny actions proposed as a response. Two simple examples: we were exhorted to take our shopping home in a reused plastic bag, and to feel good about doing so—only to be told later that the bag is responsible for about *one-thousandth* of the environmental footprint of the food it contains.[3] In the same spirit of 'every little helps', we were urged to turn off our phone chargers at night—and then it emerged that the energy thus saved was equivalent to driving a car for one second.[4]

In retrospect, our design focus on messages and things distracted attention from the system behind the thing—the societal values, and economic structures, that shaped our behaviour in the first place. We committed to *do less harm* within a system that, because it must grow in order to survive, unavoidably *does more harm* as it does so. This lesser-of-two evils approach has also compromised one of the alternative words to sustainability being proposed: 'resilience'. Described by one commentator as 'the ability to take a punch', resilience planning has resolutely evaded an

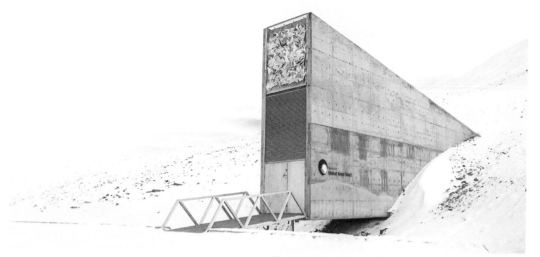

The Global Seed Vault in the archipelago of Svalbard, Norway, is a seed bank created to insure against the loss of seeds in other gene banks during large-scale regional or global crises.

obvious question: 'Why did that guy—or system—punch you in the first place?' The answer is an economic system whose core purpose is to *produce produce produce*, and *grow grow grow*.

Signals of Transformation

The good news is that, around the world, grass-roots projects are proliferating that are shaped by a different logic. This global movement contains a million active groups—and rising. Its ranks include 'energy angels', 'wind wizards' and 'watershed managers'. There are bio-regional planners, ecological historians and citizen foresters. Alongside dam removers, river restorers, and rain harvesters, there are urban farmers, seed bankers and master conservers. There are building dismantlers, office-block refurbishes and barn raisers. There are natural painters and 'green' plumbers. There are trailer-park renewers and land-share brokers. Their number includes FabLabs, hacker spaces and the maker movement. The movement involves computer recyclers, hardware remixers and textile upcyclers. It extends to local-currency designers. There are community doctors. And elder carers. And ecological teachers. Few of these groups are fighting directly for political power, or standing for election. They cluster, instead, under names like Transition Towns, Shareable, Peer to Peer, Open Source, Degrowth, Slow Food, Seed Freedom or *Buen Vivir*.

These edge projects and networks, when you add them together, replace the fear that has so hampered the environmental movement with a story of love—a joyful new story about our place in the world. In contrast to a global economy that degrades the land, biodiversity and the people that it touches, these projects signal a growing recognition that our lives are codependent with the plants, animals, air, water and soils that surround us. The philosopher Joanna Macy describes the appearance of this new story as the 'Great Turning'—and her voice is just one among many.[5] Pope Francis's recent encyclical, *Laudato Si*, for example, promotes the concept of 'integral ecology'—a reconnection between humans and nature—to 1.2 billion readers. The pope's transformational account has been echoed by the leaders of more than a billion Muslims, a billion Hindus, a billion Confucians and 500 million Buddhists.[6] The readership of these teachings adds up to seventy-five per cent of the world's population.

Of course, if everyone did what they were told by religious leaders, there'd be no sin in the world—and we're not there yet. But a paradigm shift in science is adding secular credibility to this new story. In studies at multiple scales—from sub-microscopic viruses and slime moulds to trees and climate systems—the story

US company AeroFarms explores alternative vertical-farming solutions to face the massive degree of land use implied in current food-consumption habits.

John Thackara

Following its tradition of reusing various materials, Maison Margiela introduced bin-bag-made coats for its menswear collection, Autumn/Winter 2012.

is consistent: the essence of plants, animals, air, water and the soils is to be in relationship with other life forms—including us. A single teaspoon of garden soil, it's been shown, may contain thousands of species, a billion microbes and 100 metres of fungal networks—and this hidden world does not stop there. Microbiology permeates other ecosystems, too—including our own bodies. As in the soil, so too in our stomachs, bacteria break down organic matter into absorbable nutrients. In the case of plants, nutrients are made available through their vast surface area of root systems in the topsoil and rhizosphere.[7] For Patrick Holden, the healthy topsoil, thriving with micro-organisms, which covers much of the land's surface, is in effect the 'collective stomach of all plants'. Every action we take—from feeding soil bacteria and fungi with composts or manures, to the timing of grazing and cultivation—can enhance or diminish soil life. And because microbial processes are interconnected, the health of the soil, and our own heath, are part of a single story, too.

From Parts to Wholes

It's one thing for popes and soil scientists to tell us to care for living systems—but is urging city dwellers to empathize with earthworms too big an ask? Fewer than half of us ever see or touch soil, after all. For a long time, I harboured just such misgivings—until I had an epiphany on an island in Sweden. Fifty designers, artists and architects, gathered together for a summer workshop, were asked to explore two questions: 'What does this island's food system taste like?' and 'How does this forest think?' My concern that living soil would not engage designers proved unfounded. It was like pushing at an open door: having scrabbled around the forest of Grinda like so many voles, they then staged a Soil Tasting Ceremony,[8] in which infusions from ten different berries on the island were displayed in wine glasses next to soil samples taken from each plant's location. We were invited to compare the tastes of the 'teas' and soils in silence. It was a powerful moment. Systems thinking, it seems, becomes truly transformational when combined with systems *feeling*—which is something we all crave. 'We yearn for connection with one another, and with the soul,' writes Alastair McIntosh, 'but we forget that, like the earthworm, we too are an organism of the soil. We too need grounding.'[9]

This lesson works surprisingly well in city design. When this writer meets with city planners or managers, we always start with two questions: 'Do you know where your next lunch will come from?' and 'Do you know if that place is healthy or not?' These questions help expand the design focus beyond the dry subject

The ØsterGro project is a 600m² organic rooftop garden, five floors above an old car-auction house in the district of Østerbro, Copenhagen.

Hut & Stiel have created the first urban oyster-type mushroom farm in the centre of Vienna, using used coffee grounds as soil.

of public-service delivery towards a whole-system concern with the health of places that keep the city fed and watered. Within this frame, the health of farm communities, their land, watersheds and biodiversity become integral aspects of the city's future prosperity, too. This focus on living systems acknowledges that we live among watersheds, food sheds, fibersheds (see 'From Soil to Skin', below) and food systems – not just in cities, towns or 'the countryside'.

With food, the opaque subject of living systems finally makes sense as a design space. The presence of good bread – and the microbial vitality that bread making invokes – is an especially reliable indicator that a city's food system is healthy. In dozens of major cities, real-bread pioneers are creating shorter grain chains by connecting together a multitude of local actors in ways that reduce the distance between where the grain is grown and the bread consumed: urban farmers, seed bankers, food hubs, farmers' markets, local mills and processing facilities. In London, Brockwell Bake grows heritage wheat on allotments, in school and community gardens, and with farmers close to the city.[10] As this lattice-work of activity, infrastructure and skills connects up, regional 'grain sheds' are beginning to take shape.

New distribution platforms pay an especially important role. 'La Ruche Qui Dit Oui' (The Hive That Says Yes), for example, is the brainchild of a French industrial designer and chef, Guilhem Cheron. La Ruche combines the power of the internet with the energy of social networks to bridge the gap that now separates small-scale food producers from their customers. When someone starts a local hive, they recruit neighbours, friends and family to join – the ideal number seems to be thirty to fifty members – and the group then looks for local food producers to work with. These farmers offer their products online at a desired price, and hive members pay twenty per cent on top of that to cover a fee for the hive coordinator, a service fee to La Ruche, plus taxes and banking costs. La Ruche makes money as a platform provider, but it is not an intermediary: the farmer receives the price asked for, and the system is fully transparent; everyone involved knows what happens to every cent transacted. In food platforms such as La Ruche, the focus is not just on production; they embody a whole-systems approach in which the interests of farm communities and local people, the land, watersheds and biodiversity are considered together – with stewardship as a shared value.

A focus on food systems leads to a new design agenda for cities. New kinds of enterprise are needed: food co-ops, community kitchens, neighbourhood dining, 'edible gardens' and food-distribution platforms. New sites of social creativity are needed: craft

In 2015, Architecture 00, the architecture firm behind the WikiHouse initiative, were commissioned to design and lead the community self-building of the first open-source 3D-printed WikiFarmhouse in Rugby, UK.

breweries, bakehouses, productive gardens, cargo-bike hubs, maker spaces, recycling centres and the like. Business support is needed for platform co-ops that enable shelter, transportation, food, mobility, water and elder care to be provided collaboratively—and in which value is shared fairly among the people who make them valuable.[11] Technology has an important role to play as the infrastructure needed for these new social relationships to flourish; mobile devices and the internet of things make it easier for local groups to share equipment and common space, or manage trust in decentralized ways. The most important technologies are more earthly than virtual—those to do with the restoration of soils, watersheds and damaged land. The clean-technology platform ClimateTECHwiki lists 260 promising techniques—from beach nourishment to urban forestry.

From Soil to Skin
Clothes are another daily life necessity in which alternative forms of design and production are emerging. Thanks to the tireless work of activists and researchers, millions of people are now aware of the harm wrought by textiles and fashion as industrial systems—from energy and water use to soil depletion, waste and toxic outputs from materials manufacturing. But although the fashion industry—famously sensitive to consumer attitudes—has developed sophisticated ways to measure these social and environmental impacts, exhortations to 'buy less, wash less' have proved ineffective, on their own, in an economy whose financial DNA compels it to grow at all costs. Not a single fashion brand has told its customers to buy less. Chastened, but not defeated, the new approach is to grow alternative networks at the edges of the mainstream fashion system. In California, for example, a project called Fibershed links together the different actors and technical components of a bioregional ecosystem: animals, plants and people, skills, spinning wheels, knitting needles, floor looms. For Fibershed's founder, Rebecca Burgess, the priority is to integrate vertically—'from soil to skin'. By design, the health of soils is an integral part of this whole-systems approach. Rather than constantly drive the land to yield more fibre per acre, cotton-marketing specialist Lynda Grose helps farmers match production to the capacities of the land, the health and carrying capacity of which is constantly monitored; in this way, decisions are made by the people who work the land and know it best, and fibre prices are based on yields that the land can bear, and on revenues that assure security to the farmer.[12] 'Growth' is thus measured in terms of land, soil and water getting healthier, and communities more resilient.

Earth

The Ocean Cleanup project by Boyan Slat aims to strip seventy million kilograms of plastic from the sea in ten years.

A New Story of Place

The design world has innovated a raft of alternative methods and frameworks as replacements for industrial mass production. They have names like cradle-to-cradle, natural step, living buildings, resilience planning, biomimicry, the circular economy, the symbiotic economy and the blue economy. Although welcome, these approaches are limited by a persistent blind spot: they take the 'needs of the present' – and the economic system that currently meets them – as their starting point, and proceed from there. Globalization, in particular, has distracted us from a fundamental design principle: complex phenomena cannot be isolated from their context – and no two places on the planet are the same. As explained by Joel Glansberg, a pioneer of regenerative design, ecological systems – through the forces of their geology, hydrology and biotic communities – organize themselves around certain identifiable patterns that are unique to each place. Social and cultural systems are part of the same story; woven over time through human settlement, they too are shaped by the ecology of the landscape.[13]

If the regeneration of social and ecological assets cannot be practised remotely, our design focus needs to shift from things to connections – especially the connections between people and natural systems in places that have a shared meaning and importance. Pre-eminent among these meaningful places is the bioregion. A bioregion maps the abstract concepts of sustainability, or a 'living economy', to the real world. 'The economy' becomes a place. The urban landscape is reimagined as an ecology with the potential to support us: the soils, trees, animals, landscapes, energy systems, and water and energy sources on which all life depends. A bioregional approach, which nurtures the health of the ecosystem as a whole, attends to flows, bio-corridors and interactions – inside cities, as well as in the countryside. It thinks about metabolic cycles and the 'capillarity' of the metropolis, wherein rivers and bio-corridors are given pride of place. A number of design tasks follow from this approach. Maps of a bioregion's ecological assets are needed: its geology and topography, its soils and watersheds, its agriculture and biodiversity. The collaborative monitoring of living systems needs to be designed – from soil health to air quality – and ways found to observe the interactions among them, and create feedback channels. Many of these tasks entail diverse disciplines collaborating together – with design as the 'glue' that holds them together.

The reconnection of cities to their bioregion – their 're-wilding' – is not so much about the creation of wide open spaces and new parks, it's more about patchworks, mosaics and archipelagos.

John Thackara

The self-proclaimed autonomous neighbourhood of Christiania in Copenhagen is one of the oldest-established examples of alternative self-sustainable communities in Europe.

Cover illustration by Peter Holm for the book *Inquiries into the Nature of Slow Money* (2008) by Woody Tasch, which proposes alternative economic models based on soil-production values.

When parks were built in past centuries, they were called the 'green lungs' of towns. Decades of overdevelopment have put an end to those expansive days; this new approach is all about nurturing patches, some of them tiny, and linking them together. There are cemeteries, watercourses, avenues, gardens and yards to adapt. There are roadside verges, 'green' roofs and facades to plant. Sports fields, vacant lots, abandoned sites and landfills can be repurposed. Abandoned buildings and ruins, empty malls and disused airports need to be adapted – not to mention the abandoned aircraft that, before too long, will be parked there. In Vienna, the Biotope City Foundation supports the 'micro green spaces' project for transforming neighbourhoods.[14] And in the Jaeren region of Norway, whose landscape has been battered by the footprint of the oil economy, the architect Knut Eirik Dahl teaches young designers to look for, and appreciate, the tiniest examples of biological life in among the people, goods and buildings: solitary plants, rare lichen and rare insects. It's low-cost, hands-on work. It has been called 'dirty sustainability'.

In a project called 'Dartia', for example, a coalition of statutory organizations and local people are stewarding the Dart Valley bioregion in south Devon. Based on a detailed scientific analysis of the river's social and ecological assets by the Westcountry Rivers Trust, Dartia coordinates diverse physical activities such as the repair of riverbanks; the monitoring of what's being put down drains, and the creation of rain gardens that use storm water run-off.[15] The health of soils near the river, and flora and fauna, are monitored. Drinking-water purification stations are established. Access to the water is improved for kayaks, and restricted for cows. A 'Dartia Guild' brings a wondrous variety of rivershed stakeholders together: a large estate, farms, a water-treatment plant, a plant nursery, a pub, a supermarket, a restaurant, a school, house and boat owners, a dock, and more. The guild helps the region's citizens see Dartia through new eyes and generate new ways to realize its contribution to a local living economy.

A Care Economy

In the new economy that's now emerging, *care* – for the wellbeing of social and ecological systems – replaces money as the ultimate measure of value.[16] Growth, in this care economy, takes on new meaning as the improved health of soils, plants, animals – and people – in unique social and ecological contexts. Money will not disappear as this new economy unfolds – but it will be only part of the picture. We can be confident of this because in the care-based economy that's existed throughout human history, relatively few of the ways we've looked after each other and the land involved paid-for work. Trust between people, communing, shared owner-ship and networked models of care were just as important. They will be again – enabled and strengthened by social creativity and technology. The notion of a care economy can sound poetic, but vague. Where, you may ask, is its manifesto? Who is in charge? These are old-fashioned questions. The account given by Joanna Macy – of a quietly unfolding transformation – is consistent with the way scientists, too, explain how complex systems change. By their account, a variety of changes, interventions and disruptions accumulate across time until the system reaches a tipping point: then, at a moment that cannot be predicted, a small release of energy triggers a phase shift, and the system as a whole transforms.[17]

We are in a between-two-worlds period of history. Myriad details are emerging of an emerging care economy, in which the very word 'development' takes on a profoundly different meaning to what it had before. The core value of the care economy is stewardship, rather than extraction. It is motivated by concern for future generations, not by what 'the market' needs in the next few months. This new economy cherishes qualities found in the natural world, thanks to millions of years of natural evolution. It also respects social practices – some of them very old ones – learned by other societies and in other times. This new approach to development is not backward-looking; it embraces technological innovations, too – but with a different mental model of what they should be used for. With every action we take, however small – each one a new way to feed, shelter and heal ourselves, in partnership with living systems – the easier it becomes. Another world is not just possible. It is happening, now.

1   DeLong, Brad, 'Earl Cook's Estimates of Energy Capture', *Grasping Reality with the Invisible Hand* (January 22, 2012).
2   Neva Goodwin *et al.*, 'Consumption and the Consumer Society', *Global Development and Environment Institute, Tufts University* (accessed June 6, 2016).
3   Eric Schlosser, *Fast Food Nation: The Dark Side of the All-American Meal* (New York, 2012).
4   David MacKay, *Sustainable Energy – Without the Hot Air,* (Cambridge, 2008).
5   Macy, Joanna, 'The Great Turning', *Center for Ecoliteracy* (June 29, 2009).
6   Roser-Renouf, Connie *et al.*, 'Faith, Morality and the Environment', *Yale Program on Climate Change Communication* (January 19, 2016).
7   Holden, Patrick, 'Soil is the stomach of the plant', *Sustainable Food Trust* (April 17, 2015).
8   Thackara, John, 'How does this forest think?' *Doors of Perception* (September 1, 2014).
9   Alastair McIntosh, *Soil and Soul: People versus Corporate Power* (London, 2001).
10 Forbes, Andrew, 'A New Grain Revolution', *Bread Matters* (accessed June 6, 2016).
11 Trebor Sholtz, 'Platform Cooperativism: Challenging the Corporate Sharing Economy', *Rosa Luxemberg Stiftung* (January 2016).
12 'Lynda Grose', entry, *Sustainable Cotton Project* (n.d.).
13 Joel Glanzberg, Ben Haggard and Pamela Mang, 'Looking to Nature for a New Economic Model', excerpted from *Fox Haven: Voices of the Land*, Regenesis Collaborative Development Group, Inc. (2004).
14 Andrew Taylor, 'Green space issues in a comparative perspective: Berlin, Dublin, Marseille and Turin', report for University of Helsinki (January 15, 2013).
15 'The Dart & Teign River Improvement Project: A Catchment Restoration Fund Report', *Westcountry Rivers Trust* (accessed June 6, 2016).
16 Ina Praetorius, 'The Care-Centered Economy: Rediscovering what has been taken for granted', essay for the Heinrich Böll Foundation (2015).
17 National Intelligence Council, 'Global Trends 2025: A Transformed World' (November 2008).

Christien Meindertsma
Fibre Market

Christien Meindertsma explores the life of products and raw materials. Through design, she aims to regain an understanding of processes rendered invisible by industrialization. For her first book, *Checked Baggage* (2004), Christien purchased a container filled with a week's worth of objects confiscated in Schiphol Airport after 9/11. She meticulously categorized and photographed all 3,267 items. For her second book, *PIG 05049* (2007), she used photographs to document the extensive array of products generated from the various parts of a single, anonymous pig. This book reveals lines that link raw materials with producers, products and consumers that have become invisible in a globalized world. Her work has been exhibited in MoMA, New York, the V&A, London, and Cooper Hewitt, New York.

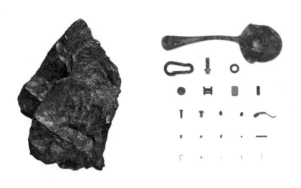

Bottom Ash Observatory, a research project with Thomas Eyck, 2014

Bottom Ash Observatory, research on the materials contained in twenty-five kilograms of bottom ash residue, 2014

PIG 05049, a research catalogue about all the products made out of a single pig, 2007

One Sheep Sweater, a collection of knitted sweaters, each bespoke-made from the wool of merino sheep, 2010

The moment someone buys a piece of cloth, they become not only its owner but the reason it exists. That monetary exchange completes the production chain. It validates the effort invested in getting the product through a lengthy and complex chain of activities to the end consumer. The buyer makes the final decision, based on how much the farming, washing, spinning, weaving, sewing, dyeing, packaging, transporting and displaying are worth. Often, this value is very low – but when the textile is discarded, its value drops below zero.

'Fibre Market' is the working title for this installation, which shows how textiles can be upcycled on an industrial scale. Until recently, it was technically impossible to automatically sort discarded textiles by their type of fibre, which has meant that they are mostly downcycled or incinerated. This installation addresses that issue, exploring the upcycling opportunities of a technique that can sort textiles in a way that allows both the fibres and their colour to be reused. It considers what happens to the value of the fibre when the production chain becomes circular instead of linear, when the endpoint of the original piece of cloth becomes the starting point of a new value chain.

The opportunities for upcycling have been largely ignored. In the Netherlands, a country with seventeen million inhabitants, 235 million kilogrammes of textiles are discarded every year – of which, 145 million are thrown out while ninety million are thrown in the recycling bin. Of the textiles that end up in the bin, about fifty-six per cent are re-wearable, thirty-seven per cent are recyclable, and seven per cent are non-recyclable. The re-wearable textiles are mostly exported to less-developed countries. The recyclable ones are cut up into cleaning rags or fibres used for mattress fillings or insulation materials. Non-recyclable textiles are burned in incinerators. Yet the production of fibres from textiles can have a huge impact on recycling opportunities, as they can be subsequently developed back into high-quality yarns and used as a resource for new products. Currently, this is not very common. In recent years, though, new processes have started to make mechanical and chemical recycling possible.

In a globalized world, we are so removed from production processes that they are almost invisible to us. But it is important to try to understand them – important for designers but also for consumers, who ultimately decide whether or not to buy a product. If we do not understand and value the journey from a product's origins to the end consumer, it is impossible to ensure that we are taking care of what lies behind it: the materials that it is made of; the places that it comes from; the energy that it takes; and, perhaps most importantly, the people who farmed, produced and transported it. Over the past decade, I have explored what lies behind a number of products. One project, 'One Sheep Sweater', consisted of a collection of sweaters made from the wool of a single sheep, while another, 'PIG 05049', comprised a catalogue of all the products made from a pig after it was slaughtered – such as sweets, heart valves and even bullets. With the 'Flax' project, I documented, together with a film-maker, an entire value chain from the flax plant to its end products. Meanwhile, 'Bottom Ash Observatory' was a project about the value of incinerated trash, which contains highly valuable resources including silver and gold.

Recently, I have become interested in how the rapid development of advanced recycling techniques is influencing these processes, and creating new opportunities. 'Fibre Market' explores this great potential through one example of mechanical recycling – Fibresort. Recently developed by the Belgian machine maker Valvan together with the Dutch textile-sorting company Wieland, Fibresort is a new technique for sorting textiles by colour and fibre type. The first Fibresort system integrated in a sorting line became operational in March 2016, but when the two companies were initially testing the machine, they were puzzled. It kept throwing pieces of clothing in the wrong bins. A sweater, for instance, would end up in a polyester bin despite its label stating that it was made of wool. It was assumed that the machine was not working properly, but, after many trials and detailed analyses, they realized that the labels were wrong. This is interesting, both from the perspective of the initial buyer of the product and the recyclers, because it means that the fibre's value may not be what it claims to be.

The starting point of the installation is discarded, recyclable sweaters – a fitting category to test the technique, because sweaters are mostly made of one kind of knitted fabric rather than a combination of fabrics, as with jackets or trousers. In the Netherlands, this category makes up six per cent of the total amount of discarded textiles, i.e. about six million kilogrammes, or eighteen million sweaters a year. Using the Fibresort technique, we will sort 1,000 sweaters by colour and fibre category, and keep a sample of each sweater with its label. I chose to focus on sweaters made of wool blends because these are the most valuable material available, and thus – an extra research dimension – the category with the highest likelihood of finding misleading labels. For the exhibition, the 1,000 woollen sweaters will be sorted by the percentage of wool in their blend (many blends also contain acrylic and nylon). They will then be sorted by colour, a new process for Fibresort. After that, various groups of sweaters – for instance, black 100 per cent wool, blue wool–acrylic mix or pink wool–nylon mix – will be pulled apart into fibres by yet another machine.

These new raw materials will be displayed in the gallery as a materialized 'bar chart' – large coloured piles of fibres. The installation aims to show the value embedded in discarded clothing, a value that can only be achieved through industrial-scale sorting. Its goal is to save the energy, time, effort and other resources – the love, for example – that have been invested in these textiles, so that they can flow into the hands of new designers and, ultimately, new owners.

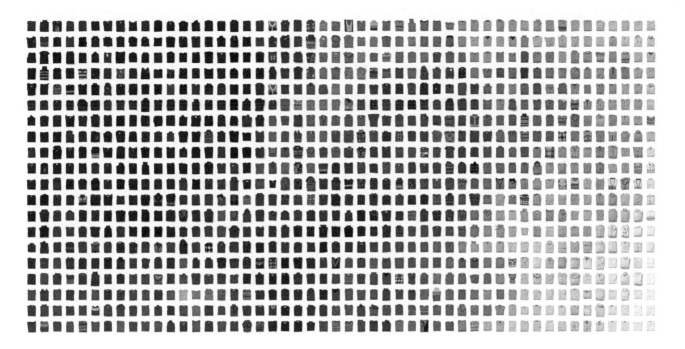

To begin her research on alternative clothing-recycling models, Christien Meindertsma collected 1,000 sweaters, which were then sorted by colour and fibre type. The simple process of sorting clothes by colour and fabric before their shredding allows the production of a much wider range of products.

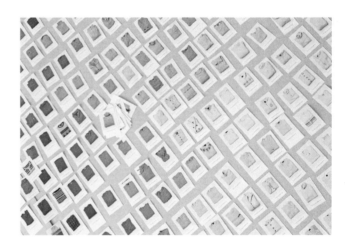

This process allows the designer to obtain a precise range of different fibres that can actually be reused for making new clothes, thus meeting consumer needs. Traditional, non-sorted clothing recycling produces a greyish, rough material that can't be used for creating new clothes, only products such as mover's blankets.

Christien Meindertsma

The 'Fibre Market' research has been developed in collaboration with various companies–including Wieland Textiles for the colour sorting and Valvan Baling Systems for the fibre-composition identification, carried out via a spectroscopic scanning of the clothes.

Christien Meindertsma in conversation with Gonzalo Herrero

GH CM

Your work is concerned with the stories behind objects, from their origins to their final destinations. What led to this interest in the whole life cycle of design?

It all started with my graduation project, where I made a series of sweaters out of the wool from one sheep. The idea was to create an industrial product while keeping the link to its origins. That meant making a product that didn't need a fake marketing story behind it – just its own honest story, which is good enough. After my graduation, I started actually doing that. I gradually found that this way of working is actually inspiring in the way that you find out things that you didn't imagine before. It's simply much nicer to be on the road, rather than just sitting behind your desk. Even though it's a time-consuming way of working, it's also a really fruitful way of finding things that you hadn't thought about before, which I think is what being a designer is very much about – about pushing boundaries.

Would you say that your practice reflects a shift in the role of the designer?

Yes, I think there has been a big change in the past ten years. Designers are not merely people making products. I think we are moving very much away from products to service design, social design and seeing designers as thinkers. Designers are operating in a much bigger field than before. But also there is less physical production happening nowadays in western Europe and North America, where designers have different tasks and different problems to solve. And a lot of the production is not in their own countries any more, which is also changing the discipline.

GH CM

Is this shift leading to a rupture between applied and theoretical designers?

A few years after graduating, I listened to Paola Antonelli at the graduation show at the Design Academy Eindhoven questioning who wanted to design a chair any more. That question reflected on this 'shift'. Traditionally, a designer was somebody who designed a product, and now there's this idea that designing a chair is somehow a bad thing. But actually, if you want to stimulate a local industry or the use of a material, it needs a product behind it – otherwise, it just keeps on being a story.

How do you balance making and research in your practice?

Even if I am working on a more theoretical project, it always means driving around a lot, talking to people, because this research is a kind of information that you can't really find on the internet or in books, or it's very new. I always try to visit everyone myself, but that takes a lot of time. When I design products – for instance, for Thomas Eyck – I explore how to produce them locally, although in this system that makes them more expensive. We work on a royalty basis, and that gives me quite a lot of freedom because I don't have to work on products on a day-to-day basis, so I can spend more time researching.

Can design influence a structural change in our consumption habits?

I've really tried to make products locally that anyone could afford, and I've realized that this is very complicated. You need a lot of people in order to do something like that, but that's the challenge: in order to make a real difference, you have to do it on a bigger scale. Sometimes people think that designers are these elitists making expensive things, but this is because if you want to make something properly the hours add up, and that increases the cost.

GH   CM

Do you think we'll see even more of a
shift from aesthetics to processes
over the coming years?

The shapes themselves will be much
more designed to be part of a chain.
Now I think that products are not made
with the idea that there is a world before
and a world after that design, and how
it is going to be circular. For instance,
in the textile industry buttons and
decorations are really problematic in
the recycling process. There's a way
to get them out of the textiles, but if we
were designing smarter then the whole
recycling process would be much
smoother. My project for *Fear and Love*
is very much about recycling, but
recycling is like the 'back door' of the
production chain—the whole process
should be much more circular.

How did the idea for 'Fibre Market'
originate?

I discovered a Dutch company that
collects second-hand clothes, and for
the past two years they have been
developing a machine that can automatically separate clothes by scanning them
and separating them. So the machine
can 'see' if it's cotton, linen, polyester,
acrylic, whatever. And it can also scan
colour, but they can't combine those
two processes yet. I asked them if they
would be interested in doing a collaborative project, and they were very
enthusiastic. From a design angle,
the possibilities of a machine that can
separate fabric are endless.
    I also found out some interesting
things. For instance, when they were
first testing the machine, they thought it
wasn't working because the labels in the
clothes would say, for instance, ninety
per cent wool, ten per cent polyester, but
the machine would keep throwing it in
the polyester bin. So they kept tweaking
it until they found out that the labels
were just lying! I found this really shocking. It's basically fraud, but of course
it's almost impossible for the consumer
to know.

GH   CM

How would you say that 'Fibre
Market' responds to *Fear and Love*?

In 'Fibre Market', I'm trying to reveal
something of the spirit of the time. It's
really changing super rapidly, how
we are treating materials and also how
we are looking at reusing materials,
because these systems are getting so
much smarter. I think that in the future
we will look back and think, 'Wow, we
had all these really beautiful coloured
textiles and we just threw them away.'
If you lived 500 years ago, you would
have found this totally outrageous.
All these colours, all these materials
—and we just burned them or threw
them away.

In a sentence, what statement does
your installation make about
design today?

By creating a landscape of wonderful,
colourful fibres, the project shows that
even the smallest bit can be reused.

The installation presents samples of shredded fibres from 1,000 discarded woollen jumpers, organized by colour.

The different fibres Meindertsma collected are catalogued on individual sheets of paper with the material labels showing. The installation aims to reveal that what we throw away is precious and that there is untested potential in upcycling clothes.

Christien Meindertsma

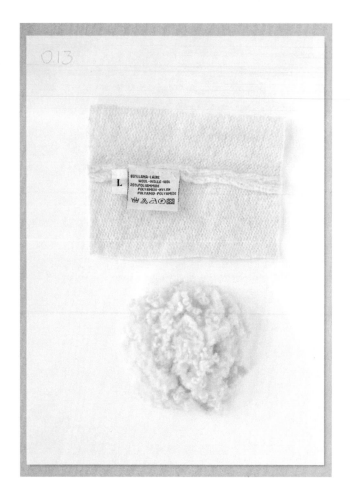

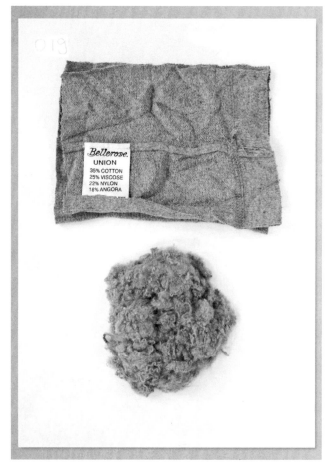

During her research, Meindertsma realized that in some cases the spectrometric scan to identify the material composition of the garments didn't match the label description. Without the right equipment, this fact hinders the process of recycling and sorting the garment by fabric type.

005

MADE IN ITALY
FABRIQUÉ EN ITALIE

60% WOLLE - WOOL
LAINE - WOL
LANA - LANA

POLYAMID
NYLON
20% POLYAMIDE
POLIAMIDA
POLIAMMIDE

15% SEIDE - SILK
SOIE - ZIJDE
SEDA - SETA

5%

Christien Meindertsma

According to a BBC report, two million tonnes of clothes are thrown out in UK every year, with only sixteen per cent being recycled. Most of that is exported to countries such as Uganda, for resale or collection in dumps where non-biodegradable clothes tamper with the soil's productivity; they stop water from entering the soil, and their run-off hampers food production.

The 'Fibre Market' installation raises awareness of the massive scale of society's fashion consumption, and the second-life upcycling potential of clothing. It also poses questions about how fashion design can be rethought, in order to create a more efficient recycling process.

Christien Meindertsma

Ma Ke
The Earth

Born in 1971, and currently based in Zhuhai, Guangdong Province, Ma Ke is one of China's most influential designers. In 2006, she founded the Wuyong Design Studio. Today, Wuyong has become a social enterprise, committed to the continuation and innovation of traditional Chinese handicrafts. In 2008, Ma Ke became the first Chinese designer to show at Paris Fashion Week, and her work has subsequently been shown around the world. In 2014, she opened the Wuyong Living Space in Beijing, for handmade products that encourage harmony with nature. A film featuring Ma Ke's work, by director Jia Zhangke, was awarded the Best Documentary Award at the sixty-fourth Venice Film Festival.

Luxurious Qing Pin collection, 2008

My Land My People collection, 2011

Wuyong Concept Home in Beijing, China, inaugurated in 2014

My Land My People collection, 2011

Ma Ke

It took me a decade – from the early 1990s, when I was fresh out of school, until the year 2000 – to realize that the world has no shortage of fashion designers capable of making trendy, elegant, sexy and sophisticated garments, but that it badly needs clothing designers. My own definitions would set fashion and clothing greatly apart. In the world of metropolitan shopping malls and high-end boutiques, there are plenty of beautiful garments whose very unpredictability make our life colourful, and stimulate desire. You are almost convinced that you can buy whatever you can imagine.

My journeys into the remote countryside, far away from urban life, led to deeper thoughts about the values of life. I am no longer satisfied by the practical and ornamental functions of clothing, nor by breakthroughs in form – much less the drive for reputation or profit. I yearn for clothing to stand as does paint to the painter or stone to the sculptor: as a language of art, which draws the audience from an appreciation of the surface to deeper thoughts. I have a strong desire to explore the mental and spiritual life of human beings. And through the works of art that have touched me deeply, I believe that the most meaningful, creative motives should arise through caring for other people. This includes love, but it is bigger than love, and it is unconditional. I believe the greatest works of art can touch the deepest human feelings, and only these works can inspire a greater self-awareness.

I am not satisfied if people only appreciate clothing that makes them happy, or is visually appealing, or serves their needs. I believe clothing could be a specific creative language, and that it has infinite possibilities for communicating ideas and shaping our behaviour. I pursue spiritual values that are in complete opposition to today's fashion trends. In fact, it is the primitive eras of human history that attract me most, when people led a life of simplicity with a respect for nature and an instinctive understanding of things. Those anonymous crafts, born of daily life and without desire for fame or profit, still resonate through the millennia, and strike the modern mind. This is the goal I have pursued: for clothing to return to its original simplicity, and to replace our overstimulated senses with more subtle sensibilities. It should uncover the extraordinary in the ordinary, for I believe that the ultimate luxury is not the price of the clothing but its spirit.

Over time, I have concluded that the role of the designer is to be the bearer of social responsibility, a seer of trends in society and an ethical leader.

After thousands of years of agricultural civilization, and 200 years of industrialization, people now possess an over-abundance of things, and yet their desires are ever harder to satisfy. This is a world in which rich and poor are increasingly polarized. Now, in the twenty-first century, we have to face a deepening environmental crisis caused by short-sightedness and a radicalization of human activity. Our resources are running out, while our desires are proliferating. Cultural variety and regional diversity are being assimilated through economic globalization. Traditional craftsmanship is disappearing from our daily lives, and can now only be found in museum exhibits. Through these tremendous social changes, my country is undergoing a heartbreaking loss of tradition for the sake of an irresponsible pursuit of 'the future'.

Albert Einstein once said that to get over a crisis you cannot rely on the same thinking that caused it. In the twenty-first century, the designer should not be encouraging consumers to follow short-term trends. The environmental crisis is only the symptom of an inner weakness. We cannot escape the consequences caused by our own short-sightedness, selfishness and greed. The only positive result of the environmental threat would be to bring the whole world together, for the first time in history, to resolve the problem together. Every one of us is an equal part of the solution, without exception. Designers, who are the creators of the living environment, must no longer isolate themselves and indulge in luxury and dreams. If you have ever seen the real world, you will realize the need for designers to take on new responsibilities. The age of individualism is coming to an end, while the age of commonality and mutual growth is beginning. This is a question of survival, and the transcendence of human nature.

As a designer, I conclude that I have the following responsibilities:

Ecological responsibility (a responsibility to the future). A designer should think about the damage to the eco-system caused by the production process, stop making environmentally unfriendly commodities, use natural resources frugally and make recyclable products for the benefit of sustainable development.

Ethical responsibility (a responsibility to the present). A designer's sensibility should be used to raise awareness. Designers have the responsibility not to over-design, but to express properly; not to overstimulate people's desires. The most admirable quality in the social role of the designer is honesty. You should not sell your soul for fame or profit.

The responsibility of passing on cultural heritage (a responsibility to the past). We live in a world abundant with the wisdom of past generations, which we should protect and pass on to future generations. Our cultural inheritance is not to be put in museums but to interpenetrate our daily lives.

Above all, my understanding of clothing and the designer's role comes from my exploration of the values of the world and human life, which has become my long-lasting creative drive. I truly believe that this pursuit of the meaning of life and spiritual values has kept me going. To create, to me, is a long process of self-cultivation, not in view of a distant goal but step by step. I am devoted to creating the most essential way of living, while pursuing the richest spiritual life.

While China's textile production accounts for nearly fifty-four of the world's total, Chinese fashion designer Ma Ke and her label Wuyong, which means 'Useless', harks back to more traditional ways of producing clothes, with local manufacturing and vernacular fabric making.

The textile industry is one of the top three water-wasting industries in China, discharging more than 2.5 billion tonnes of waste water every year. Wuyong plants and harvests its own fibres for making the fabrics used in producing their clothes, which are coloured using organic, herbal dying. In the picture, Ma Ke is taking part in a regular replanting gathering.

Ma Ke

After gaining commercial success in China with the label Mixmind, in 2006 Ma Ke focused her work on her independent label, Wuyong, which recovers traditional Chinese handcraft techniques in an attempt to make people aware of their fashion-consumption habits and the related, unsustainable manufacturing processes.

Wuyong works with local tailors, trained in traditional Chinese pattern design from inner China—a business model responding to the disappearance of local industries due to the pressure of the rapid industrial growth in other parts of the country.

Despite Ma Ke's commercial success as a fashion designer – including the design of bespoke clothing for China's First Lady, Peng Liyuan – she continues to work with highly traditional methods. Pictured here are local women working with spinning wheels and looms to produce unique, handmade fabrics.

Ma Ke

In September 2014, the Wuyong Living Space was inaugurated in Beijing. It presents lifestyle products covering all the basic necessities for a simpler and healthier lifestyle, with a more harmonious and sustainable relationship with nature. This space also hosts non-for-profit exhibitions promoting traditional Chinese folk arts and handcrafts.

Ma Ke in conversation with Gonzalo Herrero

GH   MK

The industrialization of China
in recent decades has led to a huge
growth in the consumption of fashion.
What led you to go against that
and create your label Wuyong?

The ancient sages of China warned their
descendants long ago that humankind
must have the wisdom to distinguish
between 'need' and 'want', otherwise
we will descend into a limitless quest to
satisfy our desires and this will be the
source of all kinds of suffering. From
the very beginning of creating Wuyong
– which means 'useless' – I made up my
mind to only make the things we need
in life, and not to design in order to satisfy
people's various desires or to stimulate
their cravings. Against the historical
background of a commercial society,
pursuing spiritual values is, of course,
seen as alien and unorthodox, so
I called my studio Wuyong. Knowing full
well that it's 'useless', I still take great
pleasure in it.

You found commercial success with
your first label, Mixmind. Do commercial
pressures make your ethical position
more difficult?

No. Back in 2006, when I created
Wuyong, I had already made the decision to leave Exception de Mixmind,
even though it had become the most
successful designer brand in China
(and was also the first designer brand
in the history of Chinese clothing).
The reason was that after the industry
entered a period of rapid growth,
differences of opinion arose between
me and my working partner (my former
husband). I firmly believed that the brand
should orient itself towards a niche
market, prioritizing quality over quantity.
However, my partner hoped to build
on our success and ramp up expansion
in China, in the hope of increasing
profits. My original intention in founding
Exception was to create an original
Chinese designer brand with attitude
and spirit, in order to keep to a 'designer's ideal'. This idea has been miles
apart from the overwhelming majority

GH   MK

of commercial brands, which purely
seek to maximize profit. In 2004,
Exception reached 120 stores, and as
a consequence there came a decline
in the quality of goods and service.
Since there was no way to convince my
partner, I chose to leave the first brand
that I created myself, and also left
behind the marriage.

Do you see yourself as part of
a movement of Chinese designers
rejecting rapid change and rapid
urbanization? Others might include
the architect Wang Shu.

I hadn't thought about that, my drive to
create comes purely from within. It is
always hard to repress people's yearning
to return to nature. This eternal need
seems to have no necessary connection
to the times we live in. Humankind is the
child of nature, and only when we return
to nature can we be happy in body and
mind. Nature has its own laws of operation, and if human life follows natural
rhythms then it will be harmonious and
happy; if it goes against the laws of
nature, this will inevitably damage and
corrupt the soul.

In what ways does your work continue
local traditions of making clothes?
How do local communities benefit from
your traditional production methods?

I have invited women from an ethnic
minority in the rural mountainous regions
of southwest China to the Wuyong
studio, to sit at these ancient wooden
looms, to operate the shuttles, to tread
the pedals, and to weave piece after
piece of natural cloth. Starting from
handwoven cloth, my designs need to
go through the processes of spinning,
pulling the yarn, weaving, sewing,
embroidering, dying with plant-based
dyes, and many more such operations
carried out by hand, from the simple
to the complex. Often, one or two
months are needed before being able
to weave a bolt of cloth. The finished
handwoven cloth then goes through the

long processes of design, making up a paper pattern, cutting, hand sewing, and dying with plant-based dyes, before a piece of clothing is finally ready. Clothing is ordered from Wuyong according to need. After the order has been received, one often has to wait a month or two, and if there are bad weather conditions or a lack of the materials for plant dyes then one has to wait even longer. This process, which is permeated with the feeling of a religious ritual, infuses the clothes with life. When craftswomen and craftsmen make a piece of clothing with every ounce of their attention, clothing made with such care gradually takes on a life and memory of its own.

What are the challenges of designing and making clothes this way? Do your clothes require a shift in the behaviour of the consumer? And do you think it is possible to change behaviour in a consumer society?

At the moment everybody is looking for useful things, and if the effects of something can't immediately be seen then it's often seen as useless, but there may often be a mismatch between what's useful now and the values of the future. Through these 'useless' creations I want to seek the things which are most essential in human nature, the things that people will still yearn for and that won't change, no matter what stage of economic or technological development we reach.

I really don't care whether Wuyong's handmade clothes can or can't change the consumerist behaviour of the public. I simply want to share with everybody the handmade beauty which moves and fascinates me so deeply, and to help people discover that the big brands of luxury goods are not the only option for people looking for quality. Mass-producing clothes by machine is a blink of the eye in human history compared to thousands of years of making clothes by hand. After we've lost all these techniques of handcraft, our lives will be filled with standardized goods produced on the assembly line—and some of the simple, honest joy in life will disappear with them.

Often people will ask me why, in this high-tech age, I want to dig up such out-of-date things again. I say that what

we need to revive are not these crafts in themselves, but rather the relationships between people that underlie them. If you haven't invested in something then you won't cherish it, and if there is no long process to make something then how will you appreciate the level of expense at which things are produced? This is why having lots of fashionable clothes only makes people feel that they are lacking something. The more you have, the more you feel in short supply. Handcraft can help people to restrain their consumption. It's material, but it's a kind of material with spiritual value, because you know how hard it has been to come by. It can help you to treasure things and to be satisfied, to lessen material desires. In my understanding, this is the best kind of environmentalism.

Most people are not aware of the ecological costs of the fashion industry. Is it possible to clothe the world's population in a sustainable way?

Well, why shouldn't it be possible? If people the world over can recognize that the fates of humankind and nature are bound together, and that unbridled extraction and destruction in fact harm all living things (including humankind, of course), then why can't they refuse to buy unenvironmental clothing? In fact, people really don't need many clothes: a few sets for each of the four seasons in the year is already enough, there is no need to invest much money and time into clothing.

How would you say that your work responds to the theme of fear and love?

Love is the only true need of humankind; losing love is humankind's only true fear.

The collection presented by Ma Ke in her installation
titled 'The Earth' is an ongoing research project,
presented for the first time to an international
audience at Paris Fashion Week in 2008. For this
collection, the designer counted on the collaboration
of the photographer Zhou Mi, who shot local people
from Kangding (a small village near Tibet) wearing
the collection.

Kenya Hara
Staples

Kenya Hara is a designer born in 1958. Seeing design as the universal wisdom accrued by society, he works in diverse forms of design strategy and communication. Besides working as the artistic director for Muji and Tsutaya Shoten in Daikanyama, Tokyo, Hara also sees exhibitions as central to his work. He has curated numerous exhibitions, including *Re-Design: The Daily Products of the 21st Century* (2000), *Haptic: Awakening the Senses* (2004), *Tokyo Fiber '09: Senseware* (2009), *House Vision* (2013, 2016) and *Neo-Prehistory: 100 Verbs* (2016). He is a professor at the Department of Science of Design at Musashino Art University, and his book *Ex-formation* (2016), collecting together ten years of his work with students, was published by Lars Müller Publishers. *Designing Design* (2007) and *White* (2009) have both been translated into multiple languages.

Architecture for Dogs, exhibition, 2012

Hakkin, Sake Bottle, packaging, 2000

Tokyo Fiber '09: Senseware, exhibition, 2009

HAPTIC, Takeo Paper Show, exhibition, 2004

Kenya Hara

Our staple foods are those that form the basis of the act of eating – rather than that of cooking. There are 50,000 edible species of plant and yet the staple diet of billions of people comes down to just a few grains. In Europe, people use wheat to make bread and pasta; in India, naan, chapatti and dosa are made from wheat and rice; in East Asia, rice is used to produce noodles and dough for dumplings, or eaten as it is; and in Latin America, maize is used to make tortillas. This work is an attempt to rethink these staple foods, which we don't usually pay much attention to, in order to see them afresh. It is my aim to try to present a picture of what the business of food, rendered invisible by the rise of gastronomy, is really about.

Before we call upon artificial intelligence to open the doors to a new form of human civilization, I think that we need to think about what we have been eating all this time, the things that have been keeping us alive. We take staple foods for granted but they are also the starting point for human happiness and pride.

When you are able to look at things as if for the first time, the world seems to shine and we get a new perspective. Let's take a closer look at the world's staple foods. Rather than cooking with raw grains, most people first turn them into powder, i.e. flour, then form this flour into a shape that is well suited to eating. Simply put, this is 'interface design' for ingredients. Pulverized matter can be made into any conceivable shape we want, and so the shape that each part of the world chooses to fashion their flour into can tell us a lot about the culture of that particular region.

Staple foods are close to being tasteless. In that sense, they serve a function similar to that of a receptacle that transports other ingredients, seasoned or flavoured with sauces, into our mouths. Italy, a nation with a sense of form so developed that it could produce Michelangelo, created the highly sculptural macaroni. Its design is the result of seeking a shape that had the maximal surface area so that it was quick to boil, while also allowing sauce to stick well to it.

China, the country which gave us Confucianism and Zen, developed dumpling dough and the noodle, the string-shaped interface. In Japan, a nation famed for its taste for simplicity, people didn't grind their rice as in China, but simply boiled it as it was. This remains the predominant staple in Japan, though we also have noodles that come in all different grades of thickness, such as the thick *udon* and thin *somen*. In India, people grind wheat or rice into flour, and grill or bake the dough over an open flame to produce naan, chapatti and dosa. These breads are then used to scoop up foods like curry, or else to wrap up other ingredients. In Latin America, the tortilla, produced from finely rolled dough made of ground maize, is also used to wrap up and hold other ingredients.

Then there is the matter of the traditional landscape. Generally, the image of the crops used for staple foods provides the primal countryside scene for people from those regions. In Japan, where I am from, the image of the paddy fields that produce rice is indispensible to our culture. Rice farming was brought to Japan from the Asian mainland, and Japanese culture has evolved around the rice plant. The paddy fields gave us our quintessential image of the Japanese countryside. Rice plants give us not only rice, but their stems and leaves are dried into rice straw, which is then used to make *zori* or straw sandals, straw hats, rain gear, ropes and *shime-nawa*, the rope hung with strips of white paper used for purification in the Shinto religion and for New Year's decorations. As the Japanese people structured their lives around the planting and cultivation of rice – worrying about typhoons and offering thanks to the forces of nature in the autumn, when the rice was harvested – a feeling of great awe for nature was born. Japanese people believe that the seven spirits reside in each grain of rice. Looking at golden rice fields, we see the reality that lies behind Japanese culture.

People have a tendency to think that they 'produce crops' but in fact, their life, their culture, originated amid the cycle of those crops, which flourished there because they were suited to that soil. The things we know best are often the ones we know least about. Our knowledge trembles in the face of reality. On the other hand, understanding the true nature of things is something that can bring us great joy. I've interpreted 'fear and love' as 'trembling and thrills' for this piece. The work I've produced this time has nothing to do with the kind of 'infographics' that seeks to make people understand things by replacing data with artistic expression.

Design is a dialogue with the age-old human wisdom that has accumulated in objects. For example, high-rise buildings, furniture, windows, paper, computers and computer keys are all orthogonal. The shapes of our staple foods are simpler than these, more the product of inevitability. I believe that we need to pay more attention to, for example, the thickness of noodles or the shape of a slice of bread. The human race isn't as clever as it thinks. On the other hand, our age-old wisdom is not as foolish as we might believe either.

Before we think about the food supply of the future in a rational and methodical way, we need to first rethink our understanding of the relationship between people, climate and food. This installation is an attempt to raise that point. It is not an opinion or a statement, but rather the presentation of a quiet realization. If this project can make people look at bread, at pasta, at noodles as if they are looking at those things for the first time, then it will have done its job.

These grains of wheat and rice are among the
building blocks of Western and Eastern cultures.
Understanding their role in our lives is crucial
to understanding our society.

Rice fields provide one of the quintessential images
of rural Japan. The landscape – and thus, part
of Japanese national identity – has been designed
around this staple grain.

Kenya Hara

Kenya Hara in conversation with Justin McGuirk

JM KH

How do you see your role as a graphic designer—do you consider it important for designers to raise awareness about the state of the world?

What comes to mind is the expression 'the scales falling from one's eyes', which is about seeing something without preconceptions. When you are able to look at things as if you were seeing them for the first time, the world seems to shine and everything appears new. I feel like my role as a designer is not to make people understand things, but rather to make them realize just how much they don't know.

What drew you to reflect on the idea of food for this exhibition?

The fact that it's at the heart of our everyday existence. Also, I've always found the word 'staples' really interesting. People don't eat everything in equal quantities. There are some basic foods that support our continued existence. What these 'staple foods' are in each culture, and how people eat them, is not something that we usually think much about, so I thought it would be interesting to concentrate on it.

How does your piece relate to *Fear and Love*?

Being faced by something you thought you understood and realizing you didn't really understand it at all is a terrifying sensation. It is the experience of our knowledge trembling in the face of reality. On the other hand, understanding the true nature of things is something that can bring us great joy. I've interpreted 'fear and love' as 'trembling and thrills'.

JM KH

The supply of food might be considered in some ways a design challenge—how we treat the land, how we grow crops, what we make with them, how we package and ship those things. Do you agree?

Of all the creatures on earth, humans are the only ones who purposely cultivate the things they are going to eat. Looking at all the various types of cooking there are makes food seem like something extremely complicated, but the issue of staples, I believe, draws our attention to its basic function. What I've done this time isn't infographics, isn't replacing data with artistic expression in order to try and make people understand certain things.

In the early stages of this exhibition we were thinking a lot about the systems behind design. This project alludes to those fundamental, even ancient, systems. Obviously with these grains we 'design' products (pasta or bread). Where do you think design begins and ends?

I think of design as a dialogue with the age-old human wisdom that has accumulated in objects. For example, buildings, furniture, windows, paper, computers, computer keys are all designed to be orthogonal. The shapes of the staples are simpler than these—more the product of inevitability. I believe that we need to pay more attention to, for example, the thickness of noodles or the shape of a slice of bread. The human race isn't as clever as it thinks. On the other hand, our age-old wisdom is not as foolish as we believe either.

Do you bring this kind of systemic thinking to your work as creative director at Muji?

Seeing through to the very essence of things, and then making that visible; using visualization to prompt awakening—this is what lies at the core of my design. The same is true of the art direction that I'm involved with at Muji.

Rice is an elemental aspect of Japanese culture. You argue that without rice there is no Japan. Can you say more about this, both as a citizen and a designer?

Rice cultivation came to Japan from the Asian mainland, and took root there. However, rather than seeing rice as being incorporated into contemporary Japanese culture, I think we have to see it more as a question of Japanese culture growing up around the rice plant. The image of the quintessential Japanese countryside only looks the way that it does because the land was cultivated in a certain way to make paddy fields. Rice plants give us not only rice, but their stems and leaves are dried into rice straw, which is then used to make zori or straw sandals, straw hats, rain gear, ropes and shime-nawa, the rope often hung with strips of white paper and used for purification in the Shinto religion and for New Year's decorations. The Japanese people came to care about the planting and cultivation of the rice, to be wary of typhoons and to give thanks to the great forces of nature in the autumn, when the rice was harvested. The foundation of Japanese culture can be found within the cycle of the rice harvest. Japanese people believe that the seven spirits reside in each grain of rice. Looking at golden rice fields, we see the reality that lies behind Japanese culture and that made it the way it is.

Agriculture determines the design of a nation's landscape – that grain of rice is the reason why the country looks the way it does. Yet you argue that there are thousands of other crops we could be eating. Do you imagine a different landscape?

I think there are crops that are suited to the land and the environment of a particular place, and people from that place find the scenes of those crops coming into harvest as something that feels like home. We can understand things like the attraction of food from other countries, or the particular things we find delicious on a rational level, and those things also have to do with the delights of the senses. Food from other countries sometimes appears a lot

more exciting and glamorous than the food that has its roots in our own country. However, I can't imagine rice fields ever vanishing from the Japanese soil, and I don't know if I'd be able to feel Japanese without rice as my 'motherland'.

In 1976, for the Man Transforms exhibition at the Cooper Hewitt, Smithsonian Design Museum in New York, Hans Hollein covered a table with different breads from around the world. He said that bread was design. Are you going one step further here, suggesting that design begins at the level of the grain? Or is your role in this merely to present the information and raise awareness?

I didn't see that exhibition, but my design isn't about opinions or statements. It's simply about presenting the quiet realization that the things we have been eating all this time and think we know all there is to know about, we actually don't understand at all. When something we know already appears unknown to us, that is the time when our knowledge can advance to the next level.

In a sentence, what statement does your project make about design today?

Before you think about what we can do with artificial intelligence, we should first find out what it is we've been eating throughout the ages. Our staple foods are inevitably extremely familiar to us, but also they provide the starting point for human happiness and pride.

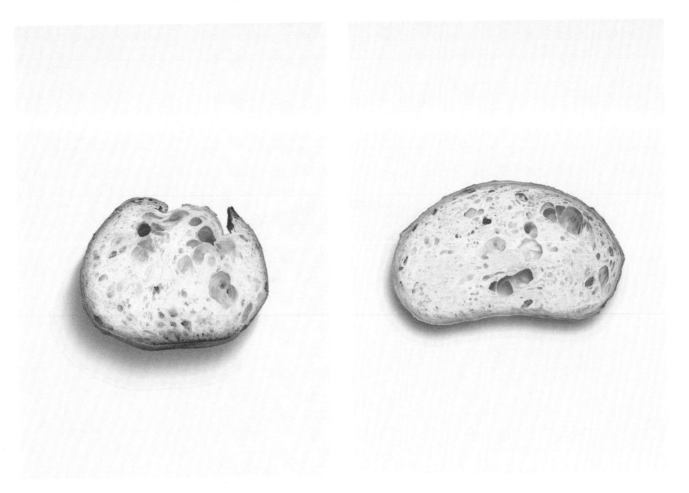

Every European country produces different breads,
but the roots of each 'design' originate in ancient
systems of agriculture and landscape that are equally
defining of their respective societies.

Earth

Japanese cuisine turns rice flour into different types
of noodle, including thick *udon* and thin *somen*.

Kenya Hara

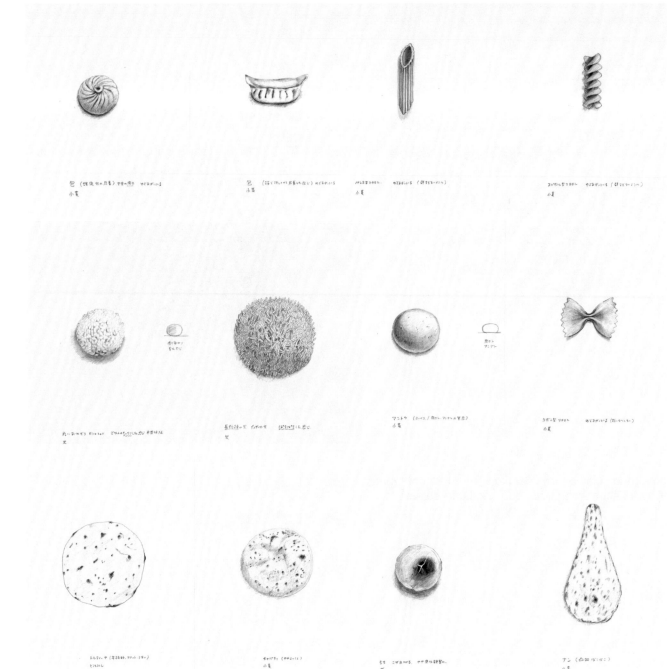

Pasta, dumplings, chapattis – these are all vessels,
relatively tasteless on their own, for other ingredients.
They are also vessels of cultural meaning.

太広麺　　　ワンタンのようをやわらかい質感。
米

　　　　　　　　　　　　　　　　　　　　　　　　　　Kenya Hara

Periphery

Neither City nor Suburb
Saskia Sassen

The periphery is a zone of ambiguous rules and orders. We did not always have peripheries, in the sense of an urban space that is neither fully part of the city nor suburban. It is a space marked by uncertain legal status. This can hold even if one's home ownership can be certified, because the underlying land might be subject to a different, much older regime from that of the building on top of it. 'Periphery' is a term that arose in Latin America to capture the vast stretches of built-up land around some of the large cities—São Paulo, Mexico City, Buenos Aires and more. But peripheries are a worldwide development in the global South.

These peripheries vary sharply across the world. If there is a feature that cuts across the differences, it is the fact of built-up terrain that ranges from reasonable to unreasonable—clearly, something we might also say about some expensively built-up city centres. The image of 'the city' as per the European tradition is not one that comes to mind. As a spatial designation, periphery is usually invoked when neither city, nor neighbourhood, nor suburb seem pertinent because it is not part of the spaces where traditional governance rules operate. Yet, there is a shape. And one question we might ask is if design can make that a better shape?

This essay documents a series of incursions into diverse aspects of peripheries. These are projects and examples of what could be done to enable a better life in what are, ultimately, spaces of hardship. I develop some of this at length, to capture the complexity of work and making that can take place in the periphery. One argument running through the piece is that design is relevant to life on the margins, to its challenges and to the emergent new types of violence. A final section focuses on the new project by China's government to aggregate what are now distinct cities into mega-regions. Notable here is the fact that the rural becomes a set of spaces *internal* to the urban, and the periphery is meant to dissolve, becoming part of central urban tissue.

Inside the Periphery
Once you enter, really enter, the periphery, many diverse worlds come to life. It looks very different than it does from an aeroplane. Yes, it is an endless stretch of low-rise built-up terrain, without green spaces, without highways and high-rise towers, without grand architecture and without statues of generals. Yet it also contains multiple differences, peculiarities, follies. At ground level, it is very much lived space.[1]

The Makoko Floating School (2013) designed by NLÉ, founded by Nigerian-born architect Kunlé Adeyemi, is a response to the unplanned urbanization of the Lagos lagoon.

Most recently, a variety of somewhat novel circumstances are engendering violence and enmities of sorts often not seen in the recent past. Behind these new kinds of violence lie factors as diverse as the drug trade and the rapid increase in the population of these peripheries, as more and more rural families are being pushed off their land by the expansion of mines and plantations.[2] The periphery, in its vastness, is one of the spaces to which the displaced can flee and become part of the tissue, not be too noticed.

Dharavi, the largest slum in Asia, was established by migrants from poor rural areas and people forcibly displaced from the centre of Mumbai, a city where nearly one person in every six lives in slums.

The periphery's living conditions are highly variable, ranging from acceptable to disastrous. Violence is one language of the disadvantaged, and it can easily become acute and murderous. Those without power often find in their neighbour a source of many evils – mostly probably unjustified. But in many situations, the neighbour is the only significant 'other' that one has access to – the politicians are very far away and the local powers, whatever their format or legitimacy, are mostly not interested in the daily sufferings of residents. So the neighbour is often 'it'.

One question that we need to ask is whether planning and design might be among a broader range of useful tools to deal with such emerging conflicts in increasingly dense settlements. It is quite important to recognize to what extent these are constructed environments, going from the physical to the relational. In focusing on the periphery, I want to understand design as a very broad variable, one that is alive and able to adapt a shape to novel circumstances.

The cable car Metrocable, part of the UN Habitat's Participatory Slum Upgrading Programme in Medellín, Colombia, connects people living in slums to the city centre.

One instance is the United Nations Habitat agency's effort to upgrade slums, more politely described as 'irregular urbanization'. Rather than engaging in slum demolition based on the absence of legal ownership, Habitat considered the possibility of in-between mechanisms. Habitat is advocating a shift in approach to slum upgrading – from thinking of slums as islands of poverty and informality to thinking of them as deprived neighbourhoods that are an integral part of the overall city system. But they are spatially segregated and disconnected, marked by an absence of streets and open spaces. This then became the focus. We might add that one concern was to contribute to the upgrading of such areas without raising the threat of evictions due to the lack of formal

Saskia Sassen

Teddy Cruz studies informal urbanization along the US-Mexican border. Here, in Tijuana, post-Second-World-War prefabricated bungalows from southern California are piled up using space frames.

legal ownership. UN Habitat hit on a simple but effective first step: upgrading the streets.

Its effort went towards maximizing the ways in which streets could contribute to the well-being and even legitimacy of a neighbourhood. It involved fixing 'streets'; naming them; making them formally recognizable; and thereby, possibly, setting up the legal infrastructure for home-ownership claims. The hope is that attaching a bit of legality to the upgraded streets might have a larger positive effect on the housing alongside the street – in other words, a basis for legalizing the houses and their ownership.

Here is a very different but also straightforward example of redesign that illustrates this mix of factors. The San Diego based architect Teddy Cruz has for many years designed interventions aimed at enabling poor communities. They are simple redesigns of what is old or about to be discarded because it is seen as useless. Cruz's designs often involve elementary processes that make a big difference. For instance, old suburban bungalows in San Diego that are slated for demolition are sometimes trucked south of the US border to Tijuana. There, Cruz devised a way of raising the houses up on stilts to maximize the available space and, importantly, creating shaded space that can be used for multiple functions, from social to economic.

The Chilean architect Alejandro Aravena has pursued a similar logic of making incomplete, rather than over-defined, interventions. His concept is to create 'half a good house' (rather than a whole bad house for the same price) for people of modest income. Here, incompleteness makes the houses affordable to these families. It provides households with core housing elements, and enables them to complete the dwelling when they want or can afford it and how they want it. The basic fact is that poor households benefit from the existence of low-priced housing.

The Often Hidden Design in a
Complex Operational Space: La Salada
La Salada is the largest informal market in Latin America. Situated on an easily accessible site in the periphery of Buenos Aires, it is both local and international, with modest and informal traders from across Latin America – it is run by both immigrants and locals.[3] La Salada is a product of the brutal neoliberal policies implemented in Argentina by former President Menem in the 1990s. Buenos Aires, now a global

Villa Verde in Constitución, Chile, is an incremental housing project by Elemental, the practice led by Alejandro Aravena, after the city was devastated by a tsunami in 2010

city once again after the sovereign default of 2001, is unusual in the clarity with which it shows the two core aspects of global city development. At one end, are the spectacular new developments that house the highly specialized economic sectors of our global information era, and at the other end, the impoverished working classes and middle classes resorting to basic survival strategies.[4]

Buenos Aires made all of this far more visible than London, New York, Paris or Tokyo did in the 1980s. In Buenos Aires, both ends of the spectrum have their emblematic sites: Puerto Madero, an old harbour redeveloped into high-end offices and commercial spaces, for the rich, and La Salada for the poor. (The rich also have less-visible zones: gated communities, far more noxious than Puerto Madero, have been multiplying.)

Even though it is under threat of demolition, La Salada shows us that design has played a role in its success and complexity. Design enabled operational effectiveness, even if informal and without recourse to laws and police. There is an interesting, and perhaps surprising, contrast here in that the dense areas where people live are marked by more anomie in their material layout. The driving force in La Salada is the fact that all the stakeholders want to make it work, and to some extent need each other. That is to say, part of the strength of the market lies in the diversity of its economic activities. It means that its entrepreneurs have to ensure a space that is functional, not overwhelmed by fights or antagonisms that can threaten the overall shared goal: the survival of one's commercial operation.

In contrast, the adjoining neighbourhood lacks this organizational motif. It is one type of space that could benefit greatly from attention to the design of that space – the way its diverse elements interrelate in what is basically a residential area. Even if homes are often also the site for small commerce, it is the home function that dominates. There are clear zones where design could help nurture and protect the residents' relationships with one another. For instance, Habitat's upgraded-streets project can generate a collective sense of pride, encouraging residents to expect better and even undertake their own improvements. Another feature that works well to build trust in low-income neighbourhoods is small terraces in front of the house, where residents can sit and get a good view of the street and other houses. Again, I see these as first steps that can mobilize residents into collective efforts.[5]

Saskia Sassen

Dharavi, the largest slum in Asia, was established by migrants from poor rural areas and people forcibly displaced from the centre of Mumbai, a city where nearly one person in every six lives in slums.

La Salada occupies a vast terrain at the southern edge of the city centre. It is the result of two processes:

The devastation of the national textile and clothing industry, when the government opened up the country to foreign firms and imports; and the large migrations from neighbouring countries – mostly Bolivians, who came in the 1990s when Argentina's cities were booming.

The Bolivian migration consisted largely of experienced workers and small entrepreneurs, who brought with them knowledge and experience. Bolivia has a long history of enormous inequality and exploitation of its indigenous people, as well as workers and small entrepreneurs – abuses that its current Morales Government has rectified to some extent. Argentina's crisis of 2001, the largest sovereign default in post World War II history, only added to the devastation of the textile and clothing sector.

La Salada became a place for informal factories and commerce, with exports to the whole continent and overall billing larger than that of the major shopping centres in Buenos Aires. This massive, collective project of informal workers, entrepreneurs and distributors developed alongside the formal economy of the new, advanced capitalism that was thriving in global cities around the world, from Buenos Aires to Dublin to Manila. Given its scale, La Salada could not remain simply a parallel 'world': it interacted and intersected with other sectors in the city's economic and social spaces, with which it had conflicts but among which it also made alliances.[6]

One key factor underlying the vast operation of La Salada is the presence of thousands of small sweatshops distributed across many of the city's neighbourhoods. The garments and the other products made in these sweatshops are then sold both in the city's fancy boutiques *and* in La Salada, often, in the latter case, for lower-income households – a pattern that I found also in New York and London in the 1980s, though not at this scale and far less visibly. Further, La Salada is part of international formal and informal trading circuits that extend to other countries in Latin America, something I did not find in the cases of London and New York. But it became a strong part of Johannesburg's vast informal market downtown after the end of apartheid, which tapped into a vast, international sub-Saharan network.

The workers at the bottom of the complex economy that became La Salada were, mostly, exploited. In the garment

Periphery

La Salada, in Buenos Aires, is recognized as the largest informal market in Latin America, employing more than 6,000 people every Tuesday and Sunday.

sector, they are thought to be mostly Bolivian immigrants. Many have come in response to perceptions of good work conditions and pay. Instead they are held in semi-slavery, often confined. This is a story that we see everywhere, in the US, in some European cities, in China, in India.

The first to denounce this semi-slavery was the neighbourhood organization Asamblea La Alameda, in one of the largest and oldest neighbourhoods of Buenos Aires, Parque Avellaneda. La Alameda took this issue up, brought some government institutions into the effort and raided buildings known to house sweatshops to free up workers and enable them to make claims. It has now set up its own cooperative garment shops under its own brand, No-Chains.

These events have led to yet another step in a trajectory of solidarity politics and capacity development. A group of young Bolivians, who basically grew up in Buenos Aires from immigrant parents, began to meet, persuaded that if the workers themselves did not organize, there was going to be no real betterment in their conditions. They formed Simbiosis, an organization that informs workers about their rights and workplace issues, and develops strategies for intervening and mobilizing, as well as organizing teach-ins and meetings. It has developed a radio programme and a publication, *Retazos*—a popular term that means 'defiance'. Out of this has come a movement that goes well beyond ensuring respect of existing law and existing workplace regulations. The project is about the active *making* of a different type of public space, using radio, teach-ins and actions to fight from the inside the perverse dynamics that tend to ghettoize social sectors and their spaces and lives.

A public realm improvement project by Jorge Mario Jauregui as part of the Favela Bairro slum-upgrading scheme in Rio de Janeiro in the 1990s

When the Periphery Winds up Inside the 'City'

China has decided to create territorial units that override the old rural-urban divide. This has meant, for instance, opening up formerly closed villages—often local, collectively owned units—and making rural areas part of larger, urban units. These will be vast territorial entities, with between fifty and 100 million residents each. They will contain their own specific versions of the periphery, but this will be a periphery not at the edges of large cities but inside a vast, multi-shape, urban 'terrain'.

The key idea from the perspective of the Chinese planners is to override the rural vs. urban distinction and to insert at least some of 'the rural' deep inside vast, urban formations.

Saskia Sassen

The village of Wencun, China, where Wang Shu and Lu Wenyu's Amateur Architecture Studio has been building new farmers' houses and refurbishing existing ones, an alternative approach to the Chinese focus on urban development.

Soweto, one of the most populous informal urban settlements in South Africa, is at the top of the agenda of the UN Habitat's slum-upgrading programme.

This would push rural economic activities to scale up and become hyper-efficient and modernized: state-of-the-art set-ups. The connective 'tissue' will be generated by the infrastructural level in these vast regions, including a broad range of transport options that will reduce time spent in transit.[7]

This socio-spatial condition is new. We have not seen this in earlier periods; thus, our existing categories cannot capture it adequately. John Friedmann identifies two, of possibly many more, key variables as critical. One is that this post-urban condition needs to be understood 'not only as a physical artifact in three-dimensional space but additionally as a densely patterned, dynamic socio-cultural, economic, and political set of interdependent systems that are constituted of tens of millions of interactive decision-making units'. These interdependent systems range from households to powerful governmental entities 'connected in various ways to each other via a fourth dimension of face-to-face and electronically mediated communications and exchanges across different scales'.[8] Vis-à-vis planning, this can open new ground but also raise problems of all sorts.

The Visual Orders 'We Know', and What We Don't See

The visual orders of the periphery, especially as seen from a distance, have become familiar to us. And yet, key aspects of these vast urban areas are often a surprise to first-time visitors. Here, I have sought to emphasize a few of those aspects as concrete economic, political and cultural dynamics that can be upgraded and redesigned. Thus, as visual order, La Salada is a place of miseries, irregularities, overcrowded spaces and many other problems. Yet, if we concentrate purely on this aspect of it we miss out on the hard work, the savvy economic sense and the intelligent design of an extremely crowded space that nonetheless works; and we miss out on the will, against all odds, to organize and set up systems to enable workers and work.

This is one path into questions about the urban condition and its diverse territories, including the peripheries that concern me here. The effort is then to understand what elements need to be developed in order to advance, and enable what the residents of these huge peripheries desire.

Today's vast urban areas contain multiple dimensions that go well beyond their visual order. Among such components are both the power projects of multinational corporations and the social projects of community groups. Each of these can belie appearances. A visual representation of rich and poor areas of a city would simply capture their physical conditions. It would fail to depict the often long tentacles of electronic connectivity that can make even poor areas into nodes on global circuits, as is the case with La Salada. The challenge is to locate and specify the full depth and behavior of these spatial conditions. In the case of the peripheries of the world, this opens up a far broader range of meanings than the purely visual order might suggest.

1   See, for example, Saskia Sassen, 'The Global City and the Global Slum', *Forbes* (March 22, 2011).

2   Saskia Sassen, Chapter 2 in *Expulsions: Brutality and Complexity in the Global Economy* (Cambridge, MA, 2014).

3   Saskia Sassen, 'La Salada: The Largest Informal Market In South America', *Forbes* (March 28, 2011).

4   This was a new trend starting in the 1990s, which led to food riots by middle-class people in Buenos Aires (a historic first) and quite a few becoming garbage pickers to survive. This combination of trends has taken place with variable levels of intensity in all cities that have gone global. I saw this process back in the early 1980s as 'peripheralization at the core', to emphasize that the same structural trends that produced those spectacular buildings also produced that growing poverty. Saskia Sassen-Koob, 'Recomposition and Peripheralization at the Core', *Contemporary Marxism* 5 (1982.), 88–100.

5   On low-income neighbourhoods in a rich city, see Saskia Sassen, 'Digitization and Work: Potentials and Challenges in Low-Wage Labor Markets', *Open Society Foundations*, and 'Open Sourcing the Neighborhood', *Forbes* (November 10, 2013).

6   For more detail on La Salada and all its ramifications, good and bad, refer to *Crisis*–a political and cultural magazine based in Buenos Aires.

7   But this is not simply Gottman's spatially understood megalopolis. This post-urban landscape is a complex, multilayered entity that is interactive and, mostly, responsive to those interactions. Gottman's notion is in part represented by more familiar developments: the so-called 'Yangtze River Delta', the 'Pearl River Delta', the Tokaido region in Japan and the emerging post-urban region centred on Mumbai.

8   H Rangan, L Porter and J Chase, *Insurgencies and Revolutions: Reflections on John Friedmann's Contributions to Planning Theory and Practice* (Oxford, 2016).

Arquitectura Expandida
Potocinema

Since 2010, Bogotá-based architecture collective Arquitectura Expandida (AXP) has explored self-building processes, both architectural and social, within public and community spaces. It works as a think tank, devoted to research around community building and the right to the city. The projects involve citizens, communities and other collectives interested in the cultural, social, political and infrastructural management of the city. The interventions assume various scales, scopes and durations, but always address the immediate needs of the community.

Casa de la Lluvia, a cultural facility in Bogotá, Colombia, 2013

El Trebol, a cultural facility in Bogotá, Colombia, 2015

Casa del Viento, a community library in Bogotá, Colombia, 2014

Urban graffiti claiming a nicer, safer and more accessible public space for the people

Arquitectura Expandida

Colombia is plagued by the problems typical of Latin American countries: extreme social inequality, poverty, unplanned urbanization, spatial segregation, racism, classism and delinquency.

For more than half a century, Colombia has been locked in an armed conflict between government forces, paramilitary units and insurgent groups – particularly the Revolutionary Armed Forces of Colombia (FARC, Fuerzas Armadas Revolucionarias de Colombia) and the National Liberation Army (ELN, Ejército de Liberación Nacional). The real victims of this conflict have been the population, millions of whom have been uprooted not just by the violence between the armed forces and revolutionary groups but also by the 'war' with the drug cartels.

As of December 2014, a shocking 5.8 million people had been displaced, according to the United Nations High Commissioner for Refugees (UNHCR), meaning that Colombia has the second highest rate of internal displacement after Syria (6.5m). Ciudad Bolívar is a peripheral district of Bogotá, built over the past forty years by various waves of rural migrants forced out of their homes by the armed conflict. No one knows exactly how many people live in this district, which was built by 'pirate' developers and residents themselves, who have even occupied hills threatened by landslides. Estimates range from 700,000 to more than a million. Ciudad Bolívar has serious socio-environmental problems linked to illegal mining, violence, drugs, armed gangs and the lack of access to culture, healthcare and education.

For decades, this district was one of the most neglected in the country – the only public spaces, schools and sport facilities were built and managed by the residents themselves. This committed community has responded to the government's lack of attention with self-built schools to offer vulnerable young people an alternative to being recruited by drug cartels or local gangs, but also the opportunity to see themselves as active participants in the making of their own neighbourhood.

In this context, violence and fear have been inherent aspects of the daily life of thousands of Colombians. Nevertheless, this long-standing situation has not dampened the optimism and stamina of the community, but has motivated them in the shared goal of transforming their situation. Arquitectura Expandida supports these processes of active and creative resistance by providing urban-planning information, and through design. We assist with self-construction, and we help manage resources to create the much-needed spaces for community meetings and other social and cultural facilities that sustain the community.

We explore construction techniques, usually with guadua (Colombian bamboo), that make self-building easier. We explore the potential of local knowledge and local initiatives, by recognizing that self-building is a cultural process. We strive to bring together the various stakeholders – both legal and illegal – who have a direct impact on the district. We explore the loopholes that allow us to exercise the citizens' right to be social and cultural managers of their own territory. And above all, we explore models of flexible organization, adapted to each context, in the quest for social city-making.

This project proposes to offer an insight into the social, political and environmental complexity of Ciudad Bolívar, where we will be actually building a school. The very difficult conditions of this context are marked by polarized feelings that could be understood as 'fear and love': on the one hand, there is the violence, poverty and lack of opportunities for the youth; on the other, there is the community's striving to improve their situation and change their fate in a creative and collaborative manner.

We are working closely with the self-managed cultural organization Instituto Cerros del Sur to build a school for audio-visual training, a process in which we are counting on the participation of the whole community. The cultural association Ojo al Sancocho already runs an audio-visual school – teaching basic film making and music making – however, it lacks a space of its own, and this new facility is intended to serve as its home. It is a place where young people can be introduced to the arts, offering an opportunity to develop skills and, potentially, careers in this sector – an optimistic alternative. And most importantly, it will provide them a space for reflection on their own neighbourhood, in which various forms of urban expression, such as graffiti and hip hop, may coalesce. Giving young people a creative outlet makes them actors in a process of change.

For the exhibition, we plan to replicate the actual structure of the school in Ciudad Bolívar. In that structure, we will exhibit the videos and other works made by students from the community in a series of workshops during the construction process. Visitors will experience the fear and love that is inherent in Ciudad Bolívar through the eyes of young people who live these emotions from day to day. The very act of displaying this participative project in the museum is a manifesto on how the future can be changed. Architecture is only one part of a process that is driven by the love of members of a whole society challenging their urban and social conditions.

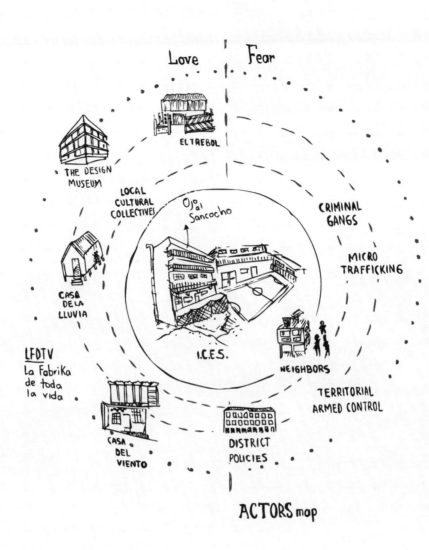

Love | Fear

THE DESIGN MUSEUM

EL TREBOL

LOCAL CULTURAL COLLECTIVES

Ojo al Sancocho

CRIMINAL GANGS

MICRO TRAFFICKING

CASA DE LA LLUVIA

I.C.E.S.

NEIGHBORS

LFDTV La Fabrika de toda la vida

TERRITORIAL ARMED CONTROL

CASA DEL VIENTO

DISTRICT POLICIES

ACTORS map

For more than thirty years, the self-managed community school Instituto Cerros del Sur has provided professional training to local young people in Ciudad Bolívar, one of the poorest, most violent and neglected districts of Bogotá, Colombia.

Arquitectura Expandida partnered with the local cinema school, Ojo al Sancocho, to build an annexe to the Instituto Cerros del Sur. Here, they can provide audio-visual training for young people in order to offer them a professional alternative that keeps them away from gangs and drug dealers.

The school is built with traditional techniques that allow neighbours to participate in the structure-assembly process, and cheap local materials to reduce building costs.

Arquitectura Expandida's mission is to work for and with the communities, to develop projects that respond to social needs and create change at different scales.

Arquitectura Expandida

Through community outreach and open assembly meetings, Arquitectura Expandida introduced their project for the annexe cinema school to the various collectives that constitute the Instituto Cerros del Sur.

The community has taken part in the open processes for designing and building the cinema school, a process that is explained in the 'Potocinema' installation (*opposite*) at this exhibition in a series of videos created by the young students at the school.

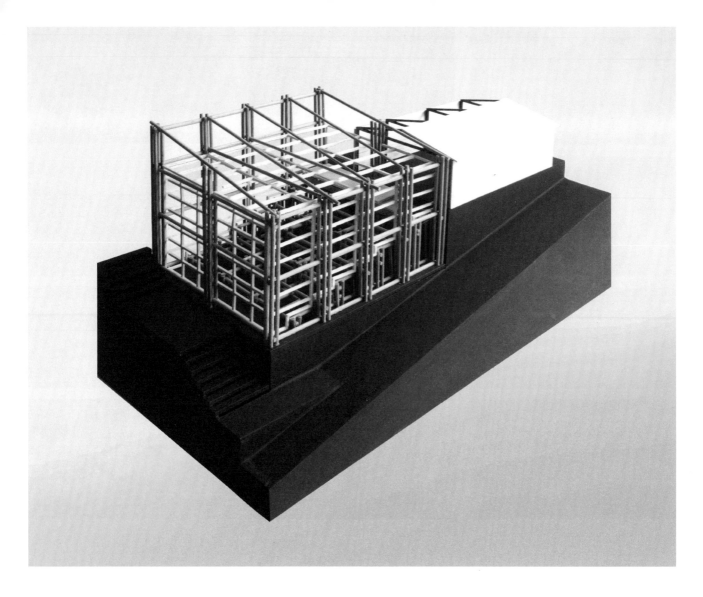

Arquitectura Expandida in conversation with Gonzalo Herrero

GH   AXP

What brought you together in
the first place?

> In 2010, two of our founding members
> organized a conference in Bogotá about
> land rights. This conference explored
> issues of urban segregation, the nature
> of informal urbanism and how architec-
> ture responds to it. Many of the city's
> construction models are extralegal and
> involve no architects, but they are local
> cultural practices and they haven't been
> acknowledged.
>   This first conference marked the
> beginning of Arquitectura Expandida,
> and established our aim of creating a
> dialogue between activists. Our work
> is based in the streets, and our practice
> focuses on actions that emphasize
> the political and educational aspects
> of self-building. For us, on-the-ground
> research is essential to understand how
> self-building projects support community
> resistance and the recognition of these
> neighbourhoods.

How do your projects with communities
benefit from you working as
a collective?

> Working as a collective allows us
> to dissolve the borders between the
> community and the rest of the stakehold-
> ers involved in a project, whether they
> are activists, artists or academics.
> This format allows us to have defined
> and common aims, those of addressing
> self-building systems and constructing
> a dialogue to promote inclusion.
> This collective format involves direct
> contact with the people. In this scenario,
> the emotive connections that are built
> between people and mutual learning are
> key elements in our work and the
> cornerstone for building our practice.

Is the collective the ultimate structure
for the future of architectural work?

> We prefer the flexibility of a collective
> model because it allows us to invent
> open organizational formats for every
> project that generate possibilities that

GH   AXP

> we neither designed nor predicted.
> This situation is very difficult to achieve
> in the closed organizational models
> typical of standard power structures, in
> which projects, actions, financing, roles
> and objectives remain entirely prede-
> fined and bureaucratically managed.
> Our activity is more like a laboratory
> that allows for alternative forms of urban
> organization. It operates under the
> premise that there is essentially no
> difference between the micro and macro
> working scales. Continuously moving
> between scales allows us to create a
> stronger platform and create a stronger,
> collaborative activist network.

Do you perceive a shift in the role
of the architect today?

> It is difficult to keep thinking of the figure
> of the creative architect as someone
> who, now turned into a social redeemer,
> is capable of posing questions and
> answering them all by themselves.
> We think of the architect as someone
> who is, first and foremost, a citizen.
> Someone able to detect critical urban
> situations, who breaks disciplinary
> boundaries and looks for joint solutions.
> An architect, in a way, who is trained in
> the streets.

How would you define fear and love
in this environment?

> Ciudad Bolivar is a neighbourhood in
> Bogotá with a population of almost a
> million, built informally in the 1980s and
> 90s. On the one hand, the fear relates
> to the armed conflict that has uprooted
> millions of people in this country, many
> of whom resettled on the periphery of
> the city, in places like Ciudad Bolívar.
> Here, fear is about surviving on a daily
> basis against the mafias who control
> the territory, the drugs and the pollution.
> The city's biggest dump is in Ciudad
> Bolívar, and the neighbourhood's land-
> scape has also been devastated at its
> rural edges by the mining industry.
> On the other hand, these controversial
> situations have given rise to a strong

local movement that can be seen as the materialization of love: love presented in the defence of human rights, access to culture, and a model of popular education as a tool of liberation.

What possibilities does architecture bring to this context and this society?

Architecture as a form of activism plays a symbolic role in the processes of resistance. It takes on a very propositional and creative character.
The strategy of self-building cultural spaces is a form of political critique. It relates to the right to the city in segregated territories in which the state has long been absent. The architecture feeds off the local area's logic and potential. It relies on self-building techniques, using local materials like *guadua*–a type of Colombian bamboo–and collective financing systems. And it allows for diverse forms of urban expression: rap, graffiti, skateboarding, community libraries, or, in our case, schools that teach audio-visual skills.

How would you say that your installation for this exhibition responds to the theme, fear and love?

Our project responds with the 'creative resistance' that we were just talking about. It addresses the possibility of strengthening a long process of social recognition across a community that exchanges technical, territorial, imaginative and life knowledge. In this way, it is linked to design and the self-building of space.

How do you expect the local community to respond to your project?

More than ten years ago, there was an idea to create a new facility for the community audio-visual school, Ojo al Sancocho. The school started inside the community itself, and has now become a priority and a necessity. This project, which is linked to the local school, the Instituto Cerros del Sur, has relied on the participation of many of Ciudad Bolívar's inhabitants from the outset. For this reason, part of the proposed 'participative' strategy is based

on trusting in the inhabitants, whom we consider to be the wisest experts on this particular territory, and in their capacity for urban self-diagnosis.
    A continuous dialogue across assemblies and cultural actors has helped us to approach and define the scopes, resources and rules of the game. Technical and budgetary limitations are always a delicate topic, but all the information is open and is accessible to all, which allows the action strategies to be jointly designed. These dynamics sometimes lead to troubled situations of open dissent. But the continuous dialogue means that the community receives this project as an opportunity to construct the territory collectively, through mutual decisions.

What statement does your installation make about design today?

Our project proposes a collective construction that is simultaneously physical, social, cultural and political.
    As the urban sociologist Robert Park once said, 'The city is man's most successful attempt to remake the world he lives in more after his heart's desire. But, if the city is the world which man created, it is the world in which he is henceforth condemned to live. Thus, indirectly, and without any clear sense of the nature of his task, in making the city man has remade himself.'

The school under construction in August 2016. Pictured here is one of the structure's most notable features: the use of tropical bamboo, known as *guadua*.

Rural Urban Framework
City of Nomads

In 2005, the Chinese Government announced its plan to urbanize half of the country's remaining 700 million rural citizens by 2030. In the same year, Joshua Bolchover and John Lin set up Rural Urban Framework (RUF), a research and design collaboration based at the University of Hong Kong. Conducted as a non-profit organization providing design services to charities and NGOs, RUF has built, or is currently engaged in, various projects in diverse villages throughout China and Mongolia. Their research explores the links between social, economic and political processes and the physical transformation of each village. Their projects integrate local and traditional construction practices with contemporary technologies.

Primary School and Educational Landscape, Mulan, 2012

Angdong Rural Hospital, Hunan, China 2014

Tongjiang Recycled Brick School, Jiangxi, China, 2012

House for All Seasons, Shijia Village, 2012

Rural Urban Framework

What does it mean to be a nomad? What does it mean to be urban? Is it possible to be a city of nomads?

These are the questions that we ask ourselves in this project, which is based on our research into recent urbanization in Mongolia. In the capital city of Ulaanbaatar, a radical urban transformation is taking place. Massive rural migration has resulted in the doubling of the urban population and an expansion of the city's territory to thirty times its original size. However, this is a people with no prior experience of collective living – there is no equivalent word for 'community' in Mongolian.

The promise of high gross domestic product (GDP) and new development projects has led nomadic herdsman to sell their livestock and move to the city in search of a better life. The result is a dense and sprawling settlement of fenced-in areas occupied by *gers* (a traditional felt tent) and other makeshift buildings. The freedom traditionally exemplified by the *ger*, pitched in the open landscape, has been replaced by an aspirational urban lifestyle as the dwelling is gradually outfitted with televisions and appliances. The *ger*, whose lightweight structure has remained unchanged for thousands of years, has suddenly facilitated one of the most rapid urbanization processes in history. It has made it comparatively easy for nomads to move to the city.

When the nomads arrive, they settle on any available land – occupying residual central areas, slopes and the periphery of the city. Once there, migrants typically erect a *ger* and surround the plot with a fence constructed from wooden posts or salvaged metal. This plot is called a *khashaa*, and each new migrant, as a Mongolian national, has the right to stake a claim to own a land parcel of 700 square metres. However, the size and rapid growth of the *ger* settlements have meant that the city has not been able to provide even the most basic services: water is fetched from kiosks, pit latrines are dug on site and garbage goes uncollected. Coal smog hovers over the city during the winter because *ger* residents burn this fuel to stay warm.

These various *ger* districts (classified as 'central', 'mid' and 'fringe' sites), represent different periods of settlement. The ones closest to the city centre are well established, with permanent houses, while those on the fringe contain the most recent migrants and are more rural in character. Within these *khashaa*, residents rear cows and pigs, and grow their own vegetables. In Chingeltei district, a mid-*ger* area, plots tend to be smaller, sometimes on steep terrain, and are cluttered with heaps of rubber tyres, scrap metal, bricks, sand or machinery parts, reflecting the shift to more urban economic activities. Many plots are starting to house more than one *ger*, either for children or to support family relatives who have just moved to the city. In others, people are transitioning from their *ger* into small houses – usually self-built, one-storey, brick and timber constructions.

This cross section of *ger* districts illustrates many of the challenges that come with urbanization. At first sight, many of them seem to be slum-like, lacking infrastructure and public spaces. However, unlike slums in other parts of the world, the residents have land ownership rights, so this is more an extreme form of suburbanization. In fact, the very notion of dividing up the land goes against Mongolian tradition, as the nomadic lifestyle was based on the collective ownership of land.

This periphery of Ulaanbaatar represents a struggle between the nomadic and the sedentary life, between the rural and the urban. Working within the extreme constraints – financial and infrastructural – Rural Urban Framework is designing prototypes that allow for the incremental evolution of the *ger* rather than its current eradication. The goal is to present a strategy for making the *ger* adaptable to modern urban lifestyles, providing a mechanism for the urbanization of Ulaanbaatar that retains aspects of the nomadic culture.

Our proposal for *Fear and Love* considers the process of transition from the rural to the urban, or from a traditional to a contemporary way of life. We identify what is positive and negative about rural and urban living. We consider the fear of losing the nomadic tradition and its freedoms versus the new challenges of fenced-in living. Both involve the need to survive in a harsh climate, but urban life brings new anxieties, new forms of insecurity and unfamiliar social behaviours. On the other hand, the nomads have traded freedom of movement for the opportunities of the city.

Our strategy in Mongolia is to transform dividing walls into a device for providing infrastructure and community programmes. In the exhibition, we explore how the *ger*, designed for an open landscape, might intersect with streets, infrastructure and other urban elements. Similarly, how can *gers* develop a more communal, public dimension? We are testing the idea of modifying this archetypal structure by conjoining multiple *gers* to create a social hub. By tackling the concept of the wall, we explore how an element that divides and contains can enable spaces of connection and community.

The battle for Mongolia's urban future highlights the intertwined instincts of *Fear and Love*, which are present in every urbanization process. Fear over the loss of tradition is countered by the hope of a better life. This is a potential conflict that we all face. The question is not only how best to urbanize, but whether we should at all?

Every year, thousands of nomads migrate to the periphery of Ulaanbaatar. Their traditional *gers* (felt tents) create instant settlements, but without any of the infrastructure required for urban life.

199

self-built house

ger - relative staying temporarily

pit latrine

coal store threshold

waste transportation driver in Khoroo

stuff

guard dog

waste ash

waste water

pile of tyres

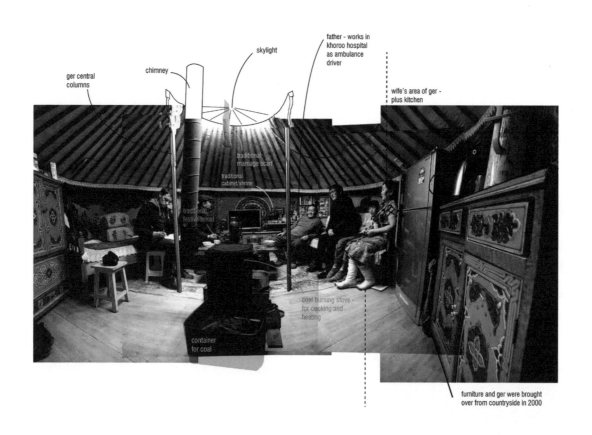

ger central columns

chimney

skylight

father - works in khoroo hospital as ambulance driver

wife's area of ger - plus kitchen

traditional marriage scarf

traditional cabinet/shrine

traditional festive bread

coal burning stove - for cooking and heating

container for coal

furniture and ger were brought over from countryside in 2000

200

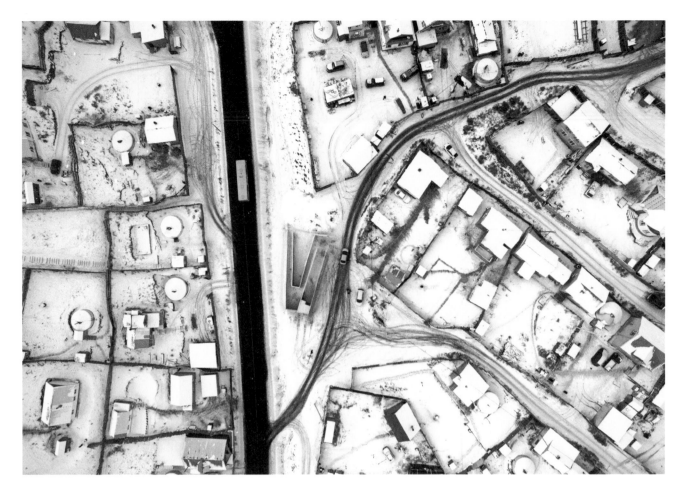

In peripheral settlements, waste simply accumulates. Since 2013, Rural Urban Framework has collaborated with The Asia Foundation and the Ulaanbaatar City Municipality to build a number of prototypes for waste disposal and collection. This one is in Chingeltei, one of nine *düüregs* (districts) of Ulaanbaatar.

Joshua Bolchover and John Lin in conversation with Justin McGuirk

JM   JB   JL

One of the interesting things about your practice is
that you have focused on rural communities in China
at a time when the rest of the world has been more
interested in the country's rapid urbanization.
Why is that?

We started working in the rural context in 2005 when
all the talk was about instant cities, speed and growth.
We really wanted to find out what was being left out,
and we found a landscape undergoing a volatile
process of transformation. So we wanted to find a role
for architects, or for architecture, in those conditions.

I would say that we had been thinking about
the transformation of the rural as the front line
of this urbanization process.

And what drew you to Mongolia?

Our research in China had been looking at the impact
of urbanization on rural areas, and in Mongolia it
became the opposite: it was the impact of these rural
migrants on the city itself.

We're fascinated by the idea that traditionally they are
nomadic herdsmen, so there's this leap from roaming
free to settling in a city. There is no equivalent word
for community in Mongolian, because they don't have
that experience of living collectively. And so,
ironically, the *ger* [traditional, circular tent]—a design
that has survived for thousands of years, and was
described by Herodotus—which allowed for freedom
of movement, is also what fuels this process of
urbanization because it allows them to move instantly
to the city.

That's true: there's not even a process of self-building
or informal construction; it's a kind of instant city.

The basic unit is the *ger* and then other things follow:
the self-building, the additions. And it's an extreme
context—Ulaanbaatar is the coldest capital in
the world. And these settlements have no sewerage,
no drinking water—every aspect is extreme. And this
offered a testing context in which to rethink what
we could do as architects who think between the
scale of the house and the urban scale.

I also just want to distinguish this scenario from slums
because, unlike most slums, these begin with land
ownership. You have the right to move your house
to a piece of land and build a fence around it. On the
other hand, there is no infrastructure—so you could
also say that it operates in a slum-like way. That's
what makes this context unique. And we were very

JM   JB   JL

interested in how we could continue to work with the *ger*, to try to plug in different kinds of domestic modules and also to try and transform it into a community space.

What are the anxieties involved here, if we talk about fear and love as a theme? You've alluded to some already, but it sounds like there is a giving up of ancestral freedom.

One issue is the fear of losing a traditional way of life. Urban life is a more generic condition, and some aspects of the traditional lifestyle are either stigmatized or slowly eroded. So it's a balance between the hope for a better life and the loss of tradition. Also, they haven't really lived among others before – so it's radically different to have a fence around your plot, rather than just having your *ger* in the steppe. It's radically different to be sedentary and not move with the seasons. So I think there's a whole process of adaptation that is still ongoing, and with it comes a degree of uncertainty about what that future might be.
        I think that we have our own inbuilt notions of what constitutes the public or the civic, and in this case I think it has to be rethought based on their lifestyles and how their way of life is changing somehow. It's difficult to put it down explicitly as 'freedom' and 'no freedom'.

Before they moved to the city, the nomadic herdsmen had collective ownership of the land because there are no individual property rights, so everyone already owns this piece of land. The idea of individual ownership only begins to appear when you move into the city and you gain property. And I think that brings a new sense of fear. I think it's also a reversal, and that's why this case is interesting: because it challenges our idea that ownership of land equals economic freedom, or a certain kind of freedom. That's a kind of aspiration we have, but here you've got a people whose lifestyle has evolved from collective ownership. This is never an issue. And actually, problems occur when you begin to own land and you stay on the same piece of land: the trash, the infrastructural problems, security issues.

Rural Urban Framework

JM   JB   JL

I'm struck by the image of a *ger* with a fence around it, and that the inherent contradiction is what is so interesting about this project. It raises questions about what is private and what is public. What are the anxieties or opportunities that come with that?

What you would assume is the most private space, inside the *ger*, is in fact the most public. We were told that when nomads wanted to have sex they would leave the *ger* and do it out in the open, and mark their spot with horse stakes to notify people to stay away. So it inverts our sense of the most private dwelling space, which is actually the space of welcoming people. The door is always open. Whereas in the city, that's no longer the case and the *ger* is surrounded by this fence.

Could you talk a little bit about your installation and how it addresses these themes?

We're asking ourselves what we, as designers, can contribute given the intensity and extreme nature of these problems; what is our role? And one of the roles that we've identified is to rethink how the *ger* and the fence begin to operate together. The fence itself has to be readdressed and redesigned. It can do more in terms of infrastructure. So thinking of ways to create new types of 'pocket' spaces or shared spaces or community spaces that readdress the fence itself.

We have an actual project in Mongolia which is re-looking at these fences, not as divisions but as opportunities for common good. We're looking at plugging in shared programmes, community programmes into this fence structure. And that's what we tried to express in the exhibition itself, which is beginning to create a common space at an intersection—so you enter this space as individuals, but you become a community. But a lot of the exhibition is about looking at the *ger* as a designed object, and rethinking that construction. Is it possible to fuse this structure, which is made for mobility and freedom and has a certain lightness to it, with other forms, or to combine several of these? These are the questions we are asking, and we are trying to use traditional elements like the felt, which is manufactured in Mongolia, working with carpenters from there to adapt them. It's a project that's about a bridge between tradition and the future. What does this have to do with fear and love? I would say that the fence is an element that is very much identified with fear—it's about division, security, containment—and we're transforming it into something that's about commonality.

...and I drop my daughter off at school before heading to work.

Time passes extremely slowly in the countryside.

Documenting the difference in lifestyle from the steppe to the city is crucial to understanding how traditional nomad architecture and customs need to adapt to urban conditions.

At the 15th Venice Architecture Biennale in 2016, Rural Urban Framework presented three adaptations of the *ger*, each proposing a way to make this ancient form relevant to contemporary urban life.

At first, the proposal was to conjoin *gers* to create a communal space (*left*), but then RUF began to think about a communal space between neighbouring *gers* (*above*).

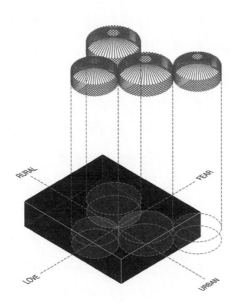

RURAL

FEAR

LOVE

URBAN

An early prototype built in Ulaanbaatar explored how an interstitial structure could connect *gers* to one another, providing a communal space and shared facilities.

Justin McGuirk is a writer and curator based in London. He is the chief curator of the Design Museum and the head of Design Curating & Writing at Design Academy Eindhoven. He has been the director of Strelka Press, the design critic of the *Guardian* and the editor of *Icon* magazine. In 2012, he was awarded the Golden Lion at the Venice Biennale of Architecture for an exhibition he curated with Urban Think Tank. His book *Radical Cities: Across Latin America in Search of a New Architecture* was published by Verso in 2014.

Bruce Sterling is an author, journalist, editor and critic, born in 1954. Best known for his ten science fiction novels, he also writes short stories, book reviews, design criticism, opinion columns and introductions for books with authors ranging from Ernst Jünger to Jules Verne. His non-fiction works include *The Hacker Crackdown: Law and Disorder on the Electronic Frontier* (1992), *Tomorrow Now: Envisioning the Next Fifty Years* (2002), *Shaping Things* (2005) and *The Epic Struggle of the Internet of Things* (2014). His most recent book is a collection of *fantascienza* (Italian science fiction) stories, *Utopia Pirata: I racconti di Bruno Argento* (2016).

JM Ledgard is a British novelist and a leading thinker on advanced technologies, risk and species survival in emerging economies. He runs his own studio, was fellow and director of a future Africa initiative at the EPFL in Switzerland, and a long-time foreign correspondent for the *Economist*. He founded the Redline cargo-drone network of roboticists, designers and logisticians to invent and build droneports and cargo-drone lines in Africa. His Redline Droneport with Norman Foster featured at the Venice Architecture Biennale, 2016. He has written two novels, *Giraffe* (2006) and *Submergence* (2011), and a collection of essays, *Terra Firma* (2015). *Submergence* is being adapted into a Hollywood film by Wim Wenders.

Susan Elizabeth Ryan PhD is professor of Art History at Louisiana State University and an affiliate of the LSU Center for Computational Technology (CCT). She teaches contemporary and new-media art history, and has helped found an interdisciplinary Art/Engineering undergraduate minor at LSU entitled AVATAR. She has lectured internationally on dress and creative technology, and has published several books in the fields of art and design history including the recent publication from MIT Press, *Garments of Paradise: Wearable Discourse in the Digital Age* (2014).

John Thackara has spent thirty years travelling the world in search of stories about the practical steps taken by communities to realize a sustainable future. He writes about these stories online, and in books; he uses them in talks for cities and business; he also organizes festivals that bring the subjects of these stories together. John is the author of the widely read blog *Doors of Perception*, and the book *How To Thrive In The Next Economy* (2015). He is a senior fellow at the Royal College of Art, a fellow of Musashino Art University and has received an honorary doctorate from Plymouth University.

Saskia Sassen is the Robert S Lynd Professor of Sociology, and co-chairs the Committee on Global Thought, Columbia University. Her recent books include *Expulsions: Brutality and Complexity in the Global Economy* (2014), *Territory, Authority, Rights: From Medieval to Global Assemblages* (2008), *A Sociology of Globalization* (2007), and the fourth fully updated edition of *Cities in a World Economy* (2011). Her books have been translated into more than twenty languages. She was awarded the 2013 Principe de Asturias Prize for the Social Sciences, and she has also been elected to the Netherlands Royal Academy of the Sciences and made a Chevalier de l'Ordre des Arts et Lettres by the French Government.

Gonzalo Herrero Delicado is an architect, curator and writer based in London. He is an assistant curator at the Design Museum. He has been a curator at the Architecture Foundation, and curated a wide range of projects in partnership with the Mies van der Rohe Foundation, Barbican Centre, Tate, Serpentine Galleries, KIA Korean Institute of Architects and SOS4.8 music festival, amongst others. His writings have been published in *Domus*, *Abitare*, *Blueprint* and *A10*.

Deyan Sudjic is the director of the Design Museum in London. His career has spanned journalism, teaching and writing. Previously he was director of the Glasgow UK City of Architecture and Design programme in 1999 and director of the Venice Architecture Biennale in 2002. He was editor of *Domus* magazine from 2000 to 2004, and founding editor of *Blueprint* magazine from 1983 to 1996. His prolific portfolio of publications includes *The Edifice Complex* (2006), *The Language of Things* (2008), *Norman Foster: A Life in Architecture* (2010), *B is for Bauhaus* (2014) and *Ettore Sottsass and the Poetry of Things* (2015). He was made an OBE in 2000.

Authors' Biographies

Note: page numbers in italics
refer to information contained
in captions.

Andrés Jaque /
Office for Political Innovation
Intimate Strangers

Design team
Andrés Jaque, Project Leader,
Roberto González, Project Leader,
Laura Mora, Sebastian Kurth,
Martín Noguerol and David Rodrigo

Research
Paola Pardo, Julie Klovstad,
Michael Nathan and Andrés Villar

Photography
Jorge López Conde and
Eduardo López Rodríguez

Sound
Jorge López Conde

Text editing
John Wriedt

In collaboration with
Grindr, Los Angeles

OMA
The Pan-European Living Room

Design team
Reinier de Graaf, Partner, OMA,
and Head, AMO, Samir Bantal,
Director, AMO, Janna Bystrykh,
Associate, OMA, Miguel Taborda,
Architect, OMA, Mario Garcia,
OMA and Filippo Mecheri, OMA

Madeline Gannon
Mimus

Design team
Madeline Gannon, Founder and
Principal Researcher, ATONATON
Julián Sandoval, Principal Designer,
ATONATON, Kevyn McPhail,
Technical Lead, ATONATON,
Ben Snell, Developer, ATONATON,
and Dan Moore, Technical
Assistance, Make It Do A Thing

With the support of
Autodesk, ABB Robotics and
the Frank-Ratchye Studio
for Creative Inquiry

Metahaven
A Love Letter to Sea Shepherd

In collaboration with
Sea Shepherd

With contributions by
Holly Herndon and Mat Dryhurst

Hussein Chalayan
Room Tone

In collaboration with
Intel

Neri Oxman
and the Mediated Matter Group in
collaboration with Stratasys Ltd.
Vespers

Research
Professor Neri Oxman,
Christoph Bader, and Dominik Kolb

Photography
Danielle van Zadelhoff

Christien Meindertsma
Fibre Market

Photography
LabadievanTour

With the support of
Wieland Textiles and Valvan Baling Systems

Special thanks to
Jessica den Hartog

Ma Ke
The Earth

Design team
Ma Ke and Shu Lei

In collaboration with
the Asian Department,
Victoria and Albert Museum

Kenya Hara
Staples

Design team
Kenya Hara, Yuka Okazaki,
Akane Sakai and Hara Design Institute,
Nippon Design Center

Illustration
Yoshitaka Mizutani

Special thanks to
Asahi Shimbun Publications Inc.

Arquitectura Expandida
Potocinema

In partnership with
Ojo al Sancocho Audiovisual School
and the people of the Potosí
neighborhood in Ciudad Bolívar, Bogotá

In collaboration with
ICES – Instituto Cerros del Sur, Vereda
Film Collective, La Fábrika de toda la
Vida collective, Belen de los Andaquies
Audiovisual School and Monstruación
Collective

With the support of
Culture Ministry of Colombia
and Cultural Office of Spanish
Embassy in Colombia

Rural Urban Framework
City of Nomads

Design team
Rural Urban Framework (RUF) and the
University of Hong Kong, Joshua Bolchover,
Principal (RUF), John Lin, Principal (RUF) ,
Ben Hayes, Project Leader (RUF), and
Josephine Saabye (RUF)

In collaboration with
GerHub: Badruun Gardi,
Dulguun Bayasgalan and Munkhbaatar
'Bodikhuu' Surenjav

Research funding provided by
the Research Grants Committee, Hong
Kong SAR, as part of the 'Incremental
Urbanism: Ulaanbaatar's Ger Settlements'
research.

This book was published in conjunction with the opening exhibition *Fear and Love: Reactions to a Complex World* at the Design Museum, London, 24 November 2016 to 23 April 2017.

Chief Curator
Justin McGuirk

Assistant Curator
Gonzalo Herrero Delicado

Project Manager
Rebecca England

Exhibitions Coordinator
Emily Durant

Senior Technician
Stuart Robertson

Curatorial Research Assistants
Yan Hong Wong and Eva Jäger

Exhibition Design
Sam Jacob Studio and OK-RM

Supported by the Embassy of the Netherlands, Creative Industries Fund NL, and AC/E Acción Cultural Española.

Additional support was provided by Autodesk, ABB Robotics, the Frank-Ratchye Studio for Creative Inquiry, Grindr, Apple, Sea Shepherd, Intel, Wieland Textiles and Valvan Baling Systems.

Special thanks to Kunle Adeyemi, Al Borde, Aric Chen, Santiago Cirugeda, Revital Cohen, Elodie Collin, Kelly Donovan, Tony Dunne, Badruun Gardi, Kate Gardner, Alexandra Daisy Ginsberg, El Ultimo Grito, Dan Hill, Anab Jain, Michelle Jocelyn, Indy Johar, Naomi Kaempfer, Bernard Khoury, Graham Lord, Luca Molinari, Julian Sandoval, Ana Naomi de Sousa, Mathew Swan, Tony Trigg, Tuur Van Balen, Ben Vickers, Julius Wiedemann, Julie Yip and Dr Zhang Hongxing.

The publishing team at the Design Museum would like to thank Ian McDonald, Robbie Penman, Polly Barton, Lisa Footitt and Julia Newcomb.

The team would also like to thank, Oliver Knight, Rory McGrath, Dewi Pinatih and Maxime Woeffray at OK-RM.

Many colleagues at the Design Museum have contributed to this book, and thanks go to them all.

Phaidon Press Limited
Regent's Wharf, All Saints Street
London N1 9PA

Phaidon Press Inc.
65 Bleecker Street, New York,
NY 10012

phaidon.com

In partnership with
the Design Museum
224–238 Kensington High
Street, London W8 6AG

designmuseum.org

First Published in 2016
© 2016 Phaidon Press Limited
Texts © 2016 the Design
Museum

ISBN 978 0 7148 7254 4

A CIP Catalog record for this
book is available from the
British Library and the Library
of Congress.

Phaidon Press Limited
Commissioning Editor
Virginia McLeod

Project Editor
Robyn Taylor

Production Controller
Mandy Mackie

Designers
OK-RM, London

the Design Museum
Publishing Manager
Mark Cortes Favis

Publishing Coordinator
Ianthe Fry

Picture Researchers
Michael Radford and
Anabel Navarro Llorens

Printed in the UK